Life After Loss

How to Deal with Grief and Bereavement after the Death of a Parent, Spouse, Child or Loved One.
(The Most Trusted Guide to Healing and Recovery)

Sheila West

Published by:

© Copyright 2021—All rights reserved.

It is not legal to reproduce, duplicate, or transmit any part of this document in either electronic means or in printed format. Recording of this publication is strictly prohibited and any storage of this document is not allowed unless with written permission from the publisher except for the use of brief quotations in a book review.

Under no circumstances will any blame or legal responsibility be held against the publisher or author for any damages, reparation, or monetary loss due to the information contained within this book, either directly or indirectly. You are responsible for your own choices, actions, and results.

Legal Notice:

This book is copyright protected. This book is only for personal use. You cannot amend, distribute, sell, use, quote or paraphrase any part or content within this book without the consent of the author or publisher.

Disclaimer Notice:

Please note the information contained within this document is for educational and entertainment purposes only. All effort has been executed to present accurate, up to date, reliable, and complete information. No warranties of any kind are declared or implied. Readers acknowledge that the author is not engaging in the rendering of legal, financial, medical or professional advice. The content within this book has been derived from various sources. Please consult a licensed professional before attempting any techniques outlined in this book.

By reading this document, the reader agrees that under no circumstances is the author responsible for any losses, direct or indirect, which are incurred as a result of the use of the information contained within this document, including but not limited to errors, omissions, or inaccuracies.

Disclaimer: Names, places, identifying characteristics and other key details may have been changed to maintain anonymity and protect privacy.

http://publish-master.activehosted.com/f/1

Table of Contents

Introduction 1

Chapter 1 5

Welcoming the New Reality 5

    Embrace Your Grief 7

    Healing Is Hardly Ever a Linear Journey 9

    Three Different Types of Grief You May Be Experiencing 10

    The Different Stages of Grief 12

    Chapter Summary 17

Chapter 2 19

Understanding How Grief Affects Us 19

    Recognizing the Symptoms of Grief 20

    What to Do When You Are Feeling Overwhelmed with Grief 25

    Write a Letter 25

    Change Your Environment 26

    Allow Yourself to Cry—Feel the Pain in All Its Fullness 26

    Spend Quality Time with Someone You Love 27

    Read an Uplifting Book or Watch an Inspiring Movie 28

    Help Someone Else 28

    Chapter Summary 30

Chapter 3 32

Tools for Channeling and Transforming Your Grief 32

    Special Release Meditation 33

    The Meditation 33

    Meditation for Self-Healing 36

    The Meditation 37

Practicing Affirmations 39

Affirmations 39

Practicing Gratitude 40

Explore an Interest or Passion... 42

Chapter Summary 43

Chapter 4 .... **45**

Understanding the Different Grieving Styles and How to Help Someone Who Is Grieving.. **45**

Gender Differences in Grieving Styles 47

How Children Grieve 49

The Dos and Don'ts of Helping a Child Grieve.. 50

Do: 50

Don't: 50

Ways In Which You Can Support a Grieving Family Member or Friend 51

Respect Their Grieving Style 52

Just Be There.. 52

Ease Their Burden 53

Practice Patience 54

Get Them Engaged in an Activity... 54

Don't Try to Fix Them.. 54

Get Them to Open Up.. 55

Make Them Laugh 56

Give Them a Gift 56

Don't Be Afraid to Mention the Deceased Person's Name 56

Things You Shouldn't Say to a Grieving Person 57

Chapter Summary 58

Chapter 5... **60**

How to Ask for Help and the Art of Receiving **60**

Why Is Asking for Help So Hard? 61

Receiving Graciously 66

Understanding The Ben Franklin Effect 67

Just Say Thank You 68

Pay It Forward 69

Chapter Summary 71

Chapter 6 73

Sorting Through the Deceased Person's Belongings and Handling Awkward Comments 73

What to Do with the Belongings of a Deceased Loved One 74

Start When You're Ready 74

Asking Yourself Important Questions 74

How Much Storage Space Do You Have? 75

Important Items that You Should Keep 76

Password Logs 76

Business-Related Documents 76

Bank Accounts/Utility Bills/Home and Other Assets Ownership/Mortgage Documents 76

Passport and Other Identity-Related Documents 77

Tax Documents 77

Retirement-Related Paperwork 77

Don't Feel Guilty about Getting Rid of Things 77

Handling Awkward Comments from Others 78

Chapter Summary 81

Chapter 7 82

Dealing With Grief Attacks and Keeping the Departed Soul Alive in Your Heart 82

Days that Are Extra Hard 83

Plan for It 83

Come Up with Creative Ideas for Celebrating the Life of Your Departed Loved One 84

Indulge in Self-Care 84

- Start a Tradition 84
- Support Groups 85
- Keeping the Departed Soul Alive in Your Heart 85
- Keep Meaningful Items with You 86
- Think About the Advice They Would Give You if They Were Around 86
- Share their Stories with Others 86
- Live Your Life in a Manner that Would Make Them Proud 87
- Finish Their Incomplete Projects 87
- Do Something from Their Bucket List 87
- Chapter Summary 88

Vanessa's Story 89

An Inspiring Account of Hope and Healing 89

Conclusion 98

I Need Your Help 100

Introduction

It was a beautiful spring afternoon—the weather was pleasantly warm and the sun was shining at its glorious best. I couldn't help but notice how beautiful the streets looked with all the trees and flowers in full bloom. Birds could be heard singing and children playing in the neighborhood. It was as if all of nature was rejoicing, yet my heart was so heavy that I was struggling to take my next breath as I was slowly walking down the street that led to the cancer hospital where my sister, Emilia, was bravely fighting for her life.

The doctors had given up. According to them, there was no hope left. All we could do was help Emilia make the most of the time she had left here on earth. I wanted to tell her how much I loved her and what she meant to me but every time I walked into that room where she was spending her last days surrounded by nurses and doctors, I struggled to speak a word.

It was painful watching her suffer so much. I prayed fervently and incessantly for her deliverance. My heart would rip apart every time I saw her tiny frame shriveled and bony after so many chemotherapy sessions. She looked nothing like the joyous, carefree, and enthusiastic woman I had known my entire life. I could still hear the ring of her laughter in my mind, but the woman in front of me was now barely able to smile.

While I had felt a profound sense of sadness for a long time watching Emilia go through these gut-wrenching trials and tribulations, something was different about that spring afternoon. I knew in my heart of hearts that something had shifted. I couldn't put my finger on exactly what it was, but I knew that things weren't the same anymore and they were never going to be the same again.

Around four thirty in the afternoon, I was sitting next to Emilia, reading a letter that my brother-in-law Charles (her husband) had written to her many years ago when he had to live away from her for a few months in a foreign country. He was desperately missing her and their children. In the letter he had professed how much he missed her beautiful smile and other small things like waking up next to her every single morning, walking hand in hand, being able to kiss and touch her. Without her, life was like a flower without a fragrance. Emilia treasured this letter because it was the ultimate testimony of their love that survived three decades against all odds.

We always marveled over how in love the two were. They were the golden couple—theirs was the kind of love that everyone aspires to and hungers for. But as luck would have it, Emilia lost her husband to lung cancer a few years ago. Emilia was devastated when Charles passed away. They had gotten married when she was eighteen and he was twenty. She had no idea how to live without him. It felt too strange, different, and unfamiliar.

In the last few months when she had entered the last stage of cancer, all she wanted to do was look at old family albums and have me read her the letters that Charles had written to her. She craved to be with him again. At times she would say, "Maybe once this is over, I will finally get to be with my husband again." Even in death, she wanted to be united with him and she was convinced that he still missed her just as much.

That afternoon, as I finished reading the letter to her, she closed her eyes with a look of deep contentment on her face. I thought she had fallen asleep, so I went outside for a walk just to refresh my mind. By the time I came back, she was gone.

How was I supposed to deal with this? I had received the most devastating news of my life. The woman who was most special to me—my best friend and dearest companion—was now gone. Until a few hours ago, I could touch her. Now, I can still touch her body but there's no one there.

Where is she? How can I talk to her again? Lord, please give me one more chance to talk to her. I have to tell her how much I love her. Oh wait, there were some other things I wanted to say. If only, I could have one more day with her, I would spend it differently. Why didn't I do those things today? Why didn't I know this was going to be the very last time I would ever see her?

I had so many regrets—so many *what if*s. Yet, the truth was she was gone. She had left for a place from where no one comes back. All I could do was learn to live again, in a world without her.

For years, I blamed myself for the things I feel I could have done better. Maybe I could have saved her if I had taken her to a different hospital. Perhaps she wouldn't have passed away that afternoon if I had kept her engaged and active.

I also felt intense anger at times—toward myself, life, God, the universe, and even Emilia. I was angry with Emilia because she came into my life, gave me so much love, and then left. Why do people enter our lives when they are eventually going to leave?

I was angry with myself for feeling the way I felt—like I had been thrown into an infinite ocean of pain and suffering. I wished my life would end because it was more alluring to stop feeling anything in death, instead of continuing to live with a broken heart.

At some point, I became weary of my pain and suffering. I just couldn't go another day like that. I craved to be happy, to smile again. I was seeking help but there weren't enough resources out there that would provide practical strategies for dealing with grief and bereavement.

It took me a long time to find the ground beneath my feet again. The saddest event of my life eventually turned into the beginning of a journey of self-discovery. While I lost Emilia, I acquired a different perspective on life and also realized that we are all here to serve in our own special way. For me, this meant helping others deal with their own grief and bereavement. I wouldn't be able to if I hadn't myself gone through the pain and suffering that comes from losing a loved one.

In the last five years, I have volunteered and worked with cancer patients. I understand what their families are going through because I have been there myself. While I can't prevent the loss of their loved ones, I can be there for them as they are coming to terms with their grief. I realized that there aren't many resources out there that offer practical advice for dealing with grief and bereavement. With this book, I am hoping to fill the hole that exists and provide you with a resource that is like a friend supporting you through these difficult times.

In the next chapter, I will help you understand this new reality that you have suddenly found yourself in. But for now, let me just say one thing: it is okay to be sad and it is okay to grieve. I am not expecting you to start jumping with joy as soon as you finish reading this book. Healing is a journey. We all need our own time to understand, accept, and embrace grief. The more you try to resist the heaviness in your heart, the more strongly it affects you. Instead, let yourself feel all those emotions you're pushing away. They will transform over time. But in order to heal from grief, you must embrace it first. I know that sounds scary, but you aren't alone. I am here to help you every step of the way!

Chapter 1
Welcoming the New Reality

> Grief is not a disorder, a disease, or a sign of weakness.
>
> It is an emotional, physical, and spiritual necessity, the price you pay for love.
>
> The only cure for grief is to grieve.
>
> —Earl Grollman

The thing with grief is that the more you try to avoid it, the worse your pain and suffering become. Grief is an intrinsic part of the human experience; it is a consequence of mortality. Life and death are two sides of the same coin. You cannot be truly alive if you fear death. In the same way, you can't fully understand and recognize the depth of your love for someone without embracing the gut-wrenching grief that comes from losing them.

When I lost my sister, I tried hard to avoid anything related to her. I was so devastated that I couldn't drive on the street where she lived. Once, I was watching a show on television and I saw a woman wearing a dress that was similar to one of Emilia's favorite dresses. That woman even had a similar stature and build to Emilia. All the good and bad memories I had with Emilia came rushing through my mind in that moment. Eventually, the memory of her death and the idea that she really was no longer around struck me like a bolt of lightning. I couldn't take it.

It was so excruciating and overwhelming that I turned the television off, and after that day I avoided watching that channel lest I might see that woman who looked so much like Emilia.

I knew that I would have to go to Emilia's house to remove her belongings so that the house could be donated to charity, as she had stated in her will. Stripping the house of her belongings was so hard that I felt like I had been punched in the gut. I wasn't ready to part with them, so I brought them over to my place and stored them in a spare room.

I couldn't bring myself to go through them. I avoided any conversation where someone might mention her. Getting reminded of my sister meant coming face-to-face with the reality that she was gone. I wasn't ready to face this truth. I tried hard to live in a bubble of normalcy, pretending as if nothing had changed.

I was also angry with her kids, my mother, and everyone else—how could they live their lives as if everything was normal? I felt like I was completely alone in my grief. No one was feeling the loss as sharply and as excruciatingly as I was. It seemed as if they had moved on while I was the only one who truly cared about her, since I was still stuck in my grief. Of course, this wasn't true, but at the time I didn't understand that everyone grieves differently. Just because we see others living seemingly normal lives doesn't mean that they aren't fighting their own internal battles constantly.

Embrace Your Grief

I know this can sound really daunting and scary, but as I stated earlier, embracing your grief is the first step on the journey of healing. You can't heal from grief if you aren't ready to accept and embrace it first.

The most important thing to understand here is that grief is a natural response to loss. It is not something anomalous or deviant that should be avoided at all costs. We can't enjoy the entire gamut of the human experience without accepting that loss and grief are intrinsically woven into the fabric of life. All of nature is pervaded with duality. That which is born must eventually die. To appreciate real happiness, we must experience sadness. To celebrate life, we must allow ourselves to mourn death.

Now, remember: while grief over the loss of a loved one is a natural experience for everyone, there are both healthy and unhealthy ways of coping. By saying that you should embrace your grief, I am not saying that you should let yourself sink into the darkness of gloom, dejection, and depression.

While it is perfectly natural to feel gloomy, dejected, and depressed every now and then when you are trying to get your life back to normal, it's not healthy if you remain stuck in that negativity for prolonged periods of time. The catch here is to feel all of those negative emotions while putting in the effort to emerge out of your grief a stronger and more loving person.

Yes, I did just say that your grief can make you a stronger and more loving person if you choose to let it transform you for the better. A lot of times people close their hearts after losing a loved one. They start thinking that love is too painful, if losing the people we love is inevitable. In my opinion, this is a very unhealthy perspective. While mourning my sister's demise, I came to this realization at some point that indeed we have very little time here on earth with the people who matter most to us. There's no telling when our meeting with someone will be the very last time we'll ever see them.

The best we can do is to live every single day with gratitude and never take anyone for granted. Coming to terms with the fact that we will never see someone who was dear to us is very painful and difficult. When I lost my sister, I really felt that I would never be happy again. The idea that I would ever be able to recover from the loss seemed preposterous and impossible.

As time passed and when I started understanding and employing a more constructive approach toward dealing with my grief, I realized that by focusing so much on who I no longer had in my life, I was ignoring those who were still around.

I really want to urge you to embrace all the emotions that come up when you get reminded of the loss you have suffered. But instead of allowing it to bog you down, let the inevitability of death be a reminder to value those who you love more than ever. Often we make the mistake of ignoring the blessings we still have in our lives when we are grieving the death of a loved one.

Healthy grieving is all about feeling the intensity of the sorrow we feel while allowing it to ease over time. No matter how grim things look right now, they will definitely improve over time. While it may seem impossible right now, eventually you will experience happiness and joy again. Of course, there will always be a hole in your life that has been left by the departure of the loved one who is no longer with you, but you can fill it with beautiful memories of that person instead of sadness, dejection, and hopelessness.

Again, to begin the healing process you have to first accept and embrace how you are feeling right now instead of trying to run away from it. It is okay to feel sad. It is okay to feel a sense of hopelessness. It is okay to not want to get out of bed some days. It is okay to wish it were all a bad dream. Don't ignore how you are feeling—accept all of the emotions that come up. Just make sure that you are simultaneously making the effort to heal and get better. You are not alone. I am here to hold your hand and guide you through each step!

Healing Is Hardly Ever a Linear Journey

The most important thing I have learned from my own experiences is that there is no universal timeline for grieving. Some people start feeling better in a matter of weeks, while others may require years to return to any sense of normalcy. You have to be extremely patient with yourself—it's just not possible to rush through the grieving process. Give yourself as much time as you need to feel better. The goal is not to stop grieving as that will happen on its own over time. Your goal should simply be to keep moving forward. As long as you are constantly making improvements, you are moving in the right direction. That's what matters most!

The other thing I want you to understand is that healing is hardly ever a linear process. One day it may seem like your pain has eased and you are feeling a sense of normalcy. The very next day, you might struggle to get out of bed. You have to embrace your feelings and emotions as they come up. There is no way to predict how you'll be feeling tomorrow, the day after, or the next week. You have to take things as they come up.

From my own experience, I can tell you that there were days when I thought life had gone back to normal. And the next week I would feel so sad and depressed that I was hardly able to function. I tried forcing myself to feel normal, but it never worked. Eventually, I stopped trying to resist the emotions that were coming up. I started living one day at a time—facing what came up moment by moment.

When you allow the process to unfold in the most natural way possible, it can be oddly beautiful. It helps you see strengths and weaknesses that you never knew you had. Indeed, there are unexpected twists and turns on the journey but they can help you realize your own truth and the truth of life itself. Losing Emilia made me question why I was here—what was the purpose of my life? When things are normal, we can get so busy just going through life that we never ask ourselves what the real purpose of our existence is. We forget how brief this experience of life really is and how transitory everything in the human experience is. Grief can bring us face-to-face with our higher spiritual self as we start realizing that we are here for something greater than just eating, sleeping, going to work, and having fun.

I used my grief for soul-searching, to find the answers to the questions that were gnawing on my soul. Hence, I emerged out of my grief a more compassionate and loving person. I realized I was here to do my bit to make this world a better place. I was here to love others with an open heart and to live every day with gratitude. Trust me, you have a higher purpose as well. While the loss of a loved one is irreparable, it can also be a gift for helping you recognize why you are here.

Grief is not a single emotion; it is a state that we go through which involves a wide range of emotions that must be felt at the deepest level possible. Over time, sadness can transform into gratitude and joy. The intensity of our grief can help us understand the depth of our capacity to love. We have to be open to what's arising out of us and fully embrace how we are feeling moment to moment. Rejecting grief is a rejection of love itself, because grief arises only when there is deep love. If you have loved once, then you can love even more deeply again. If you have been happy once, then you can be even happier again. The loss of a loved one doesn't imply the loss of love and happiness. Your loved one was a medium for bringing out what was already present in you. While that person may not be around anymore, the capacity for love, happiness, and joy is within you. It may seem hard to access right now, but trust me. You can tap into it again.

Three Different Types of Grief You May Be Experiencing

As I said earlier, different people experience grief differently. The only thing everyone has in common is the experience of loss. Some people may be able to emerge out of their grief fairly quickly (within a matter of weeks or months), while others may undergo any of these three types of grief:

Absent grief: Even though you have lost a loved one, you are feeling nothing. You're able to live your life normally and it doesn't feel like anything significant has happened. If this sounds like you, then you're experiencing absent grief.

Just because you aren't consciously feeling the grief of using your loved one doesn't mean that you didn't care for them or that there's something wrong with you. Absent grief is a defense mechanism that your brain employs to protect you from experiencing intensely negative and difficult emotions.

You may find yourself wondering why you aren't feeling anything. You are experiencing grief like anyone else who has lost someone they loved—it's just that you are coping with your loss in a different way. Over time, the latent grief may become more apparent and palpable. You just have to be patient with yourself and let things unfold naturally. Most importantly, don't let yourself feel guilty about not being visibly sad and dejected over your loss.

Delayed grief: Delayed grief usually sets in when you have first experienced absent grief. Suddenly, at some point, you come face-to-face with the magnitude and gravity of what has transpired. Your brain drops its defenses and is no longer blocking you from experiencing intensely difficult and challenging emotions.

Delayed grief may set in with full intensity all at once. Hence, you may suddenly start feeling extremely sad, remorseful, and dejected. While this is painful, it can also feel like a huge relief as you've finally come face-to-face with the real grief that had been buried inside all this time.

Chronic Grief: A lot of people suffer from chronic grief. They find it impossible to move on with their life after the loss of a loved one. This could imply remaining stuck in a sense of denial about what has transpired. Some may struggle to function normally in life.

Chronic grief doesn't just take a toll on the one suffering from it but also on the people around them as they may feel lost as to how they can help the grieving person.

If you are suffering from any of these three types of grief, it can be enormously helpful to speak to someone you trust or seek professional help. Both delayed and chronic grief can be extremely difficult to cope with and I have seen many people struggle to function normally in their daily lives. While absent grief may not seem like much to worry about, it often strikes suddenly and with a vengeance in the form of delayed grief. Hence, seeking help early may prevent delayed grief from hitting you with full force.

The Different Stages of Grief

Before we begin with a detailed discussion about the different stages of grief, I want to emphasize once again that everything takes time. You have to be extremely forgiving and compassionate toward yourself. You must give yourself plenty of space to come to terms with the gravity of the loss you have suffered and the wide range of emotions it has triggered in you. Be extremely patient and gentle with yourself. Even though your wounds are not visible, they aren't any less serious than the wounds one gets by being physically hurt. Worse still, when a person is physically wounded, everyone can see what they are going through. But when it comes to mental, emotional, and spiritual wounds, only the person suffering from grief can feel it.

Others can't understand what you are dealing with unless you tell them about it. Don't shy away from asking for help—the people who care about you will be happy to know how they can make things better for you. You must also be as cautious and gentle with yourself as you would be if you'd been physically wounded.

While at times it may seem like you have entered a bottomless pit with no hope for redemption, trust me, things will eventually change for the better. Understanding the 5 Stages of Grief™[1] can help you immensely in retaining the hope for a better tomorrow.

---

[1] Elisabeth Kübler-Ross Limited Family Partnership. 2020. Trademark covers the categories of downloadable podcasts in the field of grief, death, and dying, change management, life passages, and emotional and spiritual growth; video and audio recordings on cassettes, DVDs, compact discs, records and in digital format in the field

The 5 Stages of Grief™ model was introduced by Swiss American psychiatrist, Elisabeth Kübler-Ross, who discussed it extensively in her 1969 book, *On Death and Dying*. The inspiration for her book came from working closely with terminally ill patients.[2] She was able to closely observe how losing a loved one impacts people. In the midst of despair and grief, every person thinks that no one has endured as much suffering as them. However, the truth is that there are a lot of similarities in how people grieve.

Knowing about and understanding the 5 Stages of Grief™ can help you feel less alone as you realize that there are others who have experienced the same emotions that you are going through. No matter how hopeless you may feel right now, you will get to the next stage of grief and, with time, your pain will become less intense.

The 5 Stages of Grief™ consist of:

1. **Denial**, or denying the truth of what has happened,
2. **Anger**, or feeling angry when the truth finally begins to set in,
3. **Bargaining**, desperate attempts to try and undo the present situation,
4. **Depression**, or feeling hopeless and despondent, and
5. **Acceptance**, coming to terms with the truth and finding peace in the changed reality.

It is important to note that going through the 5 Stages of Grief™ is hardly ever a linear process. You may switch from one stage to another—constantly going back and forth—in a matter of days or even hours or minutes. For example, you could be angry for a few hours, and then you may feel completely depressed. The depression may transform into denial after another hour. Hence, you can't predict exactly which

---

of grief, death, and dying, change management, life passages, and emotional and spiritual growth. Registration no. 6147861, filed on October 30, 2017, and issued on August 5, 2020.

[2] "Five Stages of Grief." Wikipedia. Wikimedia Foundation, October 31, 2021. https://en.wikipedia.org/wiki/Five_stages_of_grief#cite_note-5.

stage you'll experience next, but it helps to know that most of the emotions a grieving person experiences can be divided into these five categories. You can also tell when things are improving as you start accepting the reality for what it is. Just don't forget that it is okay to flip from one stage to another not just in weeks or hours but also in a matter of minutes.

Now, let us explore each of these stages in detail:

Denial: The shock of the tragedy is so hard to bear that the individual struggles to accept reality for what it is. The world doesn't make sense anymore, as the foundation of the individual's life has been shaken to its core. Some people feel completely numb, while others actively make efforts to escape the reality of the loss. They may avoid all places, things, and people associated with the deceased loved one. In a lot of ways this stage is a blessing that nature bestows upon grieving individuals, as it only lets in what an individual may be able to handle at one time, while blocking out all thoughts and emotions that could overwhelm them.

There is no strict timeline for how long this stage may last, but as the sense of denial begins to start fading and the individual is able to embrace the reality for what it is, you can be sure that the healing process has started. We can't heal from something without first facing it. Hence, even though denial is an important stage in the 5 Stages model, real healing begins once denial starts to fade and reality becomes harder to escape from.

Anger: Once a person starts stepping out of denial, they feel increasingly frustrated and angry with the situation. Their anger may start targeting people in close proximity. It is normal to have thoughts like, "Why me?" "What have I done to deserve this?" and "Why has this happened?"

It's not easy dealing with intense anger and frustration. But suppressing it can make matters worse. The best way of dealing with these difficult emotions is by channeling them into something productive. For instance, you can release your anger and frustration by working out intensely in the gym.

Avoid saying anything you'd regret later by not reacting in the heat of the anger. When you are struggling to contain your anger and frustration, excuse yourself from the company of others and do something to effectively channel your anger. Moving the body is one of the best ways of releasing anger, or any negative emotion, for that matter.

Bargaining: During this stage you may seek some kind of a deal or truce. For instance, you may try bargaining with God, a higher power, or the universe to spare your loved one. In other words, you want to turn back time. You want go back to the moment that changed your life forever and have a different outcome. Of course, no one can turn back time, but it's hard to accept the truth for what it is. You can't help but hope against hope.

It is easy to become lost in an endless series of *what if*s and *if only*s. Guilt is often a close companion to bargaining. You may feel regret for the things you could have done differently. Maybe if you had taken your loved one to a different doctor, they'd still be alive, or if you had tried that new therapy, they might have survived longer. You may also find yourself bargaining with the pain itself, "I'd do anything to not feel the pain from this loss."

It is easy to remain stuck in the past, wishing you had made different choices. However, the reality of the situation is different now. It is irreversible. Be gentle with yourself—don't blame yourself for the things that weren't your fault.

Depression: At some point, we start seeing reality for what it is. It gets hard to continue to deny the truth and try to make bargains with reality. This is when you start feeling the full intensity of your grief as it settles in a form of depression.

At this stage, you may feel as if you're stuck in an endless black hole. It is normal to think that you are never going to be happy again and that this depressive state is going to last forever. It is very important to understand that depression born from grief doesn't indicate the presence of any mental illness. This kind of depression is a normal, even appropriate, response to losing a loved one. A lot of the time in our modern world, people look at this stage as something unnatural or something to immediately snap out of. That's really a terrible misunderstanding of the grieving process. There is nothing wrong with feeling depressed when your life has been turned upside down. The only time it starts becoming a matter of serious concern is when you remain stuck in the depressive state for a significantly long period of time and it severely impairs your ability to function normally in life. At that point, seeking professional help becomes a necessity.

If you have only recently lost your loved one, don't be too harsh on yourself or judge the depressive feelings. It is okay and even normal to feel lost in a maze of sadness. You may find yourself questioning the meaning and purpose of your life—all this is perfectly normal!

Acceptance: You may never feel completely okay with the fact that your loved one is no longer in your life, but you start to accept the current reality for what it is. You may still feel a hole in your heart and your life that no one can fill, but you are ready to start moving forward with your life. You are no longer fighting with, or trying to escape from, the reality of the situation.

A lot of times people want to keep living the way they did while their loved one was in this world. This may not be viable and with time they start accepting that their world has changed permanently and forever. Through growing acceptance, one can become far more appreciative about the blessings that they still have in their life and also for the presence of other loved ones who are still around.

Chapter Summary

1. You cannot be truly alive if you fear death. In the same way, you can't fully understand and recognize the depth of your love for someone without embracing the gut-wrenching grief that comes from losing them.

2. The most important thing to understand is that grief is a natural response to loss. It is not something anomalous or deviant that should be avoided at all costs. All of nature is pervaded with duality: That which is born must eventually die. To appreciate real happiness, we must experience sadness. To celebrate life, we must allow ourselves to mourn death.

3. To begin the healing process, you have to first accept and embrace how you are feeling right now instead of trying to run away from it. It is okay to feel sad. It is okay to feel a sense of hopelessness. It is okay to not want to get out of bed some days. It is okay to wish it were all a bad dream. Don't ignore how you are feeling; accept all of the emotions that come up. Just make sure that you are simultaneously making the effort to heal and get better.

4. The goal is not to stop grieving, as that will happen on its own over time. Your goal should simply be to keep moving forward.

5. Healing is hardly ever a linear process. One day it may seem like your pain has eased and you are feeling a sense of normalcy. The very next day, you might struggle to get out of bed. You have to embrace your feelings and emotions as they come up.

6. Grief is not a single emotion—it is a state that experience, which involves a wide range of emotions that must be felt at the deepest level possible. Over time, sadness can transform into gratitude and joy. The intensity of our grief can help us understand the depth of our capacity to love.

7. Rejecting grief is a rejection of love itself, because grief arises only when there is deep love. If you have loved once, then you can love deeply again. If you have been happy once, then you can be happy again. The loss of a loved one doesn't imply the loss of love and happiness. Your loved one was a medium for bringing out what is already present in you.

8. Absent grief is a defense mechanism that your brain employs to protect you from experiencing intensely negative and difficult emotions. Over time, the latent grief may become more apparent and palpable. You just have to be patient with yourself and let things unfold naturally.

9. Delayed grief usually sets in when you have first experienced absent grief. Suddenly, at some point, you realize the magnitude and gravity of what has transpired. Your brain drops its defenses and no longer blocks you from experiencing intensely difficult and challenging emotions.

10. A lot of people suffer from chronic grief. They find it impossible to move on with their life after the loss of a loved one. This could imply remaining stuck in a sense of denial about what has transpired. Some may struggle to function normally in life.

11. If you are suffering from absent, delayed, and/or chronic grief, then it can be enormously helpful to speak to someone you trust or seek professional help.

12. The 5 Stages of Grief™ are: denial, anger, bargaining, depression, and acceptance. It is important to note that going through the 5 Stages of Grief™ is rarely a linear process. You may switch from one stage to another frequently, in a matter of days, hours, or minutes.

Chapter 2
Understanding How Grief Affects Us

> I will not say: do not weep; for not all tears are an evil.
>
> —J.R.R. Tolkien, The Return of the King

We are complex beings experiencing complex emotions in our day-to-day lives. Grieving is a complex state to be in. There's really no right or wrong way to grieve. We must allow it to run its full course. More often than not, grief allows us to face hidden strengths and weaknesses that we had no clue we possessed. For instance, losing my sister to cancer got me to develop a special kind of compassion for other people like her. I started volunteering actively with terminally ill cancer patients. In some ways, I felt that by helping others like my sister, I would be able to redeem the irreparable loss I had suffered.

I would not be able to understand what those patients and their families face if I hadn't lost my own sister to cancer. Once I accepted the gravity of my loss and came to terms with the fact that I would never see my sister again, I decided to direct my energy toward helping others. In a lot of ways, this was a selfish move. Even though I was helping others, I was primarily motivated by the desire to ease my pain. But grief brought out this immense compassion and love that I was capable of giving to others.

At the same time, it brought me face-to-face with many of my inner demons. I could no longer avoid the fact that I had serious abandonment issues. Since childhood, I have always felt that I lose the people I love. This often makes me afraid to become too invested in new relationships. Recognizing that this is an issue for me has helped me a great deal in overcoming my fears.

Of course, when you encounter your inner demons, you have two choices. You can either let them overpower you or you can use them to become a stronger and even more wonderful person. As Bruce Lee said, "Do not pray for an easy life, pray for the strength to endure a difficult one."

Recognizing the Symptoms of Grief

While individual styles of coping with grief may differ (we'll discuss this subject in detail when we get to Chapter 4), there are a lot of symptoms that are common to most people. The list below is definitely not a comprehensive one, as it's simply not possible to include every single symptom of grief that different people may suffer from. Instead, I have focused on compiling a list that includes the most commonly experienced symptoms. So let us explore what they are!

1. **Crying:** You feel vulnerable and emotional. Even a small remark can trigger a strong emotional response in you. You're often on the verge of tears, especially whenever you get reminded of your deceased loved one.

2. **Headaches:** I suffered from severe headaches for months after my sister's death. My head and sinus area felt heavy from all the incessant thoughts and crying. A lot of people I have worked with

have also mentioned how their migraines got a lot worse after the death of a loved one.

3. **Difficulty Sleeping/Insomnia:** Getting a peaceful night's sleep becomes something terribly elusive when you are struggling to come to terms with your new reality without your loved one. You may find yourself desperately yearning to fall asleep—your body is too tired and exhausted—yet you aren't able to fall asleep for anything in the world.

4. **Questioning the Purpose of Life:** Losing someone who is dear to you can completely shake the foundation of your life. You may start questioning why you are still here when your loved one is gone. I know that for me one of the biggest questions was why do people come in our lives only to leave at a certain point. Death also confronts us with the temporal nature of life and all human experiences. If we give in to despair, then everything can start seeming meaningless. But then, life isn't about finding meaning—it is about giving meaning to what you have and what you want to make of yourself and of your life.

5. **Questioning Your Spiritual/Religious Beliefs (e.g., your belief in God):** Losing a loved one can leave you feeling angry with God or whatever higher power you believe in. It can truly shake the foundation of your religious and spiritual beliefs as you come to terms with the inevitability of death. However, holding on to your religious/spiritual path will serve you in the long run. People with a religious or spiritual practice feel less alone and overwhelmed by challenging life circumstances. Even if you don't consider yourself religious or spiritual, you can benefit from practices like meditation, affirmations, incantations, and the like.

6. **Feelings of Detachment:** In the face of a life-altering loss, you may feel completely lost and detached from everyone or everything. It's okay to feel this way and this doesn't make you a bad person in any way. This is actually your brain's way of protecting you from feeling more negative emotions than what you are capable of handling. Don't worry—it won't last forever. Just keep moving

forward—show up for yourself and those who matter most to you. Don't allow this feeling of detachment to let you abandon your responsibilities. Of course, if you are feeling overwhelmed by your responsibilities right now, then talk to someone who can share the load with you. A lot of times we don't get the help we desire simply because we don't ask for it. Most of the time, our loved ones would really like to help us but they may not have any idea how they can do it.

7. **Isolation from Friends and Family:** This point ties in with the previous one. You may feel completely alone in your grief and suffering. It is also common for grieving individuals to feel that no one in this world can understand what they are going through, especially because everyone has a unique way of dealing with loss and pain. Don't assume that no one can understand you. Instead, share your feelings and thoughts with those who truly care about you. Again, most of our loved ones are eager to help—it's just that they may not know how to do it.

8. **Abnormal Behavior:** If you find yourself unconsciously or compulsively engaging in any form of abnormal behavior, seek help by talking to someone you trust. It can be anything from waking up in the middle of the night to gorge on large amounts of food to not eating for days. In short, if you feel that your attitude and actions are veering on the self-destructive end of the spectrum, you may be at a point where professional help is necessary.

9. **Excess Worry and Anxiety:** If you are always so worried, anxious, and perplexed that it has become hard for you to function efficiently in your daily life, then you may need to do something to consciously relax your mind and body. Regular meditation or having any kind of spiritual practice can be really helpful for channeling this kind of negative energy.

10. **Frustration:** It is natural to feel frustrated, hopeless, or angry in the face of a life-altering loss. Just be patient with yourself and try to not let your emotions get the better of you.

11. **Guilt:** Many people feel guilty about not having done enough for their deceased loved one. You may find yourself thinking that if you had done a few things differently, your loved one may still be around. Guilt is not a constructive emotion. It drains your energy and leaves you feeling negative. Besides, you did the best that you were capable of with the knowledge and understanding that you had at the time. If you feel you have made significant mistakes that you would like to amend, then focus on helping others who are still around and whose lives you can positively impact.

12. **Fatigue:** Grieving is often an extremely taxing process—it takes a heavy toll on the mind and body. Hence, you may feel fatigued and exhausted most of the time. Be gentle and kind to yourself. Don't try to push yourself too much. You may have to opt out of strenuous activities or anything that requires a great deal of energy to accomplish.

13. **Anger:** As discussed in the previous chapter, it is okay to feel angry about the situation. You may have angry outbursts every now and then or you may feel a lot more irritable compared to your old self. Try to not direct this anger toward others who don't deserve it. Engage in physical exercise to release the accumulated emotional energy.

14. **Loss of Appetite:** You may not feel like eating at all or there may be a significant reduction in your appetite. It's really quite normal and most people who are grieving the loss of a loved one go through it. However, after a while it becomes really important to maintain a healthy and wholesome diet. Make sure that you are eating on time even if you are eating small portion sizes. Maintaining a regular eating and sleeping schedule can also help tremendously with the recovery process.

15. **Sudden Weight Loss or Gain:** This goes hand in hand with the previous point. Loss of appetite may lead you to consuming too little food which can cause significant weight loss. Many people also turn to overeating as a way of filling the physical, mental, and emotional hole that has been created by the death of their loved one.

This can obviously lead to weight gain. Again, employing healthy coping strategies like sharing your thoughts and feelings with your loved ones or working with a therapist can really help avoid these scenarios. Food is fuel for the body—don't allow yourself to abstain from it or overindulge in it because of uncontrolled emotions.

16. **Nausea:** For months after my sister's death, I felt this sinking feeling at the bottom of my stomach every time I would get reminded of her. It left me feeling nauseated and quite literally sick to my stomach. This is often a common experience among people grieving the loss of a loved one.

17. **Stress:** All the negative emotions like anger, frustration, guilt, anxiety, and so on can manifest in the form of accumulated stress. You may find it too hard to relax. I would strongly suggest that you create a list of activities that you truly enjoy doing. When you are feeling too stressed, turn to this list and find something you can do right away. This really helped me when I was grieving and it has worked for almost everyone I have worked with.

18. **Aches and Pains:** The accumulated stress and negative emotions can show up as aches and pains in the body. Stretching and getting regular massages can really help with them.

19. **Lowered Immunity:** When you are constantly stressed and overwhelmed with negative emotions, your immune system isn't functioning all too well. This can make you susceptible to coughs, colds, infections, and the like. It is very important that you actively work on maintaining a healthy diet, a regular exercise regimen, and some kind of practice to relax yourself. Be sure to also step outdoors and spend time in the sun. Spending time in nature is undoubtedly one of the best strategies for overcoming depressive thoughts and boosting overall mood.

What to Do When You Are Feeling Overwhelmed with Grief

Now that you understand some of the most important symptoms of grief and how you can handle them, let us discuss another scenario. There are times when you feel like you just can't go on anymore. You are so overwhelmed that even getting out of bed starts feeling like the hardest thing to do. I am going to give you some practical advice for handling these kinds of situations based on what has proven effective for me personally and for others I have worked with.

Write a Letter

There is something extremely cathartic about expressing your feelings on paper. There have been times when I started writing with a heavy heart how much I was hurting but by the time I finished, I felt like a different person.

You can address this letter to your deceased loved one if you are feeling desperate to talk to them. You can also address it to yourself or to no one. Just write down whatever it is you are feeling. There is no right or wrong way of doing this. The point is to get out of your system whatever it is that's bothering you. Once you have taken it all out on paper, you will immediately start feeling lighter and better.

I would strongly recommend that you burn this letter or dispose of it in some way. There is something alchemical about this process. It is a ritualistic release that immediately brings about a shift at the energetic level.

I personally like to burn the letter first and then I release the ashes in a nearby stream. I do this whenever I have pent-up emotions that feel overwhelming to me. Every single time, without fail, I feel better after going through this process. Give it a try—I'm absolutely sure you'll benefit from it.

Change Your Environment

Our external environment is, in many ways, an expression of our internal mind. Hence, changing the external environment has a powerful influence on our internal mental and emotional state. Now, there are two things you can do. Either you can remove yourself temporarily from the physical space where you are experiencing all of these negative emotions. For example, you can go to a café you really like, spend time at a friend's house, or simply go for a walk in nature. The point is to not remain confined in the same space where you are feeling mentally and emotionally stuck.

On the other hand, you can rework your space in some way. Perhaps just rearrange the furniture or move around the décor a bit. If your space is cluttered, then you definitely want to work on clearing that clutter first. It is very easy to allow our environment to become cluttered when we are going through a difficult time mentally and emotionally. Every time I clear clutter away, I feel lighter and livelier. I acquire greater clarity of mind and it always feels like I am able to breathe more easily.

I know that this idea requires a bit more effort than the previous one, but if you can give yourself the push, it will be very rewarding. You don't have to pick just one out of the two—you can try a combination of both. Changing the environment can mean inviting someone over into your physical space. This can also remarkably shift the energy of the space and help you feel better despite being in the same house.

Allow Yourself to Cry—Feel the Pain in All Its Fullness

Sometimes the best thing you can do for yourself is to let yourself cry. I know that many people would find an advice like this blasphemous. Society sees crying as something negative that must be avoided at all costs. This is such a myopic understanding of one of the most natural human emotions.

Through tears, we release a lot of our sadness and grief. Holding them back implies keeping the grief and sadness stored deep inside you. It is bound to create more problems than crying would.

Here's what I would suggest you do: Set a day aside when you'll let yourself cry as much as you possibly can. On this day, you don't have to do anything except let yourself feel sad and dejected. If you don't want to get out of bed and take a shower, then so be it.

It is important to stop running away from what you are feeling or look at it as a problem to be solved. On this appointed day, you'll simply be present with your grief and sadness. Just make sure that you don't have any important appointments or commitments scheduled on that day.

Now, you can't make a habit out of this, or it would completely defy the purpose of this mourning day. If you're going to go in full mourning for one entire day, then you must resolve to come out of it the next day. I'm not saying that you have to do anything dramatic to feel better the next day. I am sure that by the next day, you would start feeling at least a little bit lighter. So after a mourning day, it would be time to start going about the business of life again.

Spend Quality Time with Someone You Love

Love is indeed the most powerful force in the universe. Love can move mountains, so it can definitely help you heal your heart. You have lost one person that you deeply loved. But I am sure there are others in this world who hold a special place in your heart as well.

Quite often we become so immersed in our grief that we forget to value and cherish those loved ones who are still around. If you are feeling overwhelmed with grief and sadness, then reach out to someone you love. I know that a lot of people say that to reduce our grief, we should share our pain with others. I feel this can create a very tricky situation. It is all too easy to create a situation where people start feeling sad and negative. There are better ways of handling grief than sharing your negative thoughts and feelings with others. I am going to empower you with a lot of practical tips and tools in the next few chapters.

For now, I am suggesting that you spend some quality time with your loved one. Don't talk about what's bogging you down. Instead, do something together that you both enjoy. This will help you shift your focus from the sense of lacking, dejection, and sadness that you are feeling by thinking about the demise of your loved one, to one of gratitude for those beautiful souls who are still present in your life.

Read an Uplifting Book or Watch an Inspiring Movie

Reading an uplifting book or watching an inspiring movie can really help shift your frame of mind. There is no shortage of high-quality self-help material in the market—pick something that appeals to you.

I personally love watching the movie *The Shawshank Redemption*. To me, that movie represents the power of hope and never giving up, no matter how hopeless the circumstances may seem. The protagonist of the movie has to crawl through 500 yards of sewage to emerge victorious on the other end. I feel that symbolically represents the challenges that we have to go through in life. Most people give up as soon as they hit even the tiniest road bump. But if you want to achieve greatness, you have to face great challenges with determination and alacrity.

Help Someone Else

One of the best ways to get your mind off your own problems is by helping someone else. Every person believes that their burden is the heaviest, but when you start really looking around, you realize that there's so much in your life to be grateful for.

At the spiritual level, we are all part of the same cosmic whole. Therefore, it is not surprising that helping someone else feels so good and uplifting. In essence, by helping someone else, you are helping yourself. You don't have to take my word for it. Just do it and see how you feel.

Also, most people think that they need to do something big in order to feel like they are helping someone. Both big and small gestures have their place. The small things matter just as much as the big ones do. If all you can do is bake a cake for your ninety-year-old neighbor who lives alone, then do that. No act of kindness is too small or insignificant. Every good act that is done with noble intention matters and makes the world a better place for everyone.

Chapter Summary

- There's really no right or wrong way to grieve. We must allow it to run its full course. More often than not, grief can bring us face-to-face with hidden strengths and weaknesses that we had no clue we possessed

- When you encounter your inner demons, you have two choices. You can either let them overpower you, or you can use them to become an even more wonderful and stronger person.

- Losing someone who is dear to you can completely shake the foundation of your life. You may start questioning why you are still here when your loved one is gone

- If we give in to despair, then everything can start to seem meaningless. But life isn't about finding meaning—it is about giving meaning to what you have and what you want to make of yourself and of your life.

- Holding on to your religious/spiritual path will serve you in the long run. People with a religious or spiritual practice feel less alone and overwhelmed by challenging life circumstances. Even if you don't consider yourself religious or spiritual, you can benefit from practices like meditation, affirmations, incantations, and the like.

- If you are feeling overwhelmed by your responsibilities right now, then talk to someone who can share the load with you. A lot of times we don't get the help we desire simply because we don't ask for it. Most of the time, our loved ones would like to help us, but they may not know how they can do it or that we need it.

- Don't assume that no one can understand you. Instead, share your feelings and thoughts with those who truly care about you. Again, most of our loved ones are eager to help.

- If you feel that your attitude and actions are veering on the self-destructive end of the spectrum, you may be at a point where professional help is necessary.

- Many people feel guilty about not having done enough for their deceased loved one, but guilt is not a constructive emotion. It drains your energy and leaves you feeling negative.

- You may have angry outbursts every now and then, or you may feel more irritable compared to your old self. Try to not direct this anger toward others who don't deserve it. Engage in physical exercise to release the accumulated emotional energy.

- Create a list of activities that you truly enjoy doing. When you are feeling stressed, turn to this list and find something you can do right away.

- It is important that you actively work on maintaining a healthy diet, a regular exercise regimen, and some kind of practice to relax yourself. Be sure to also step outdoors and spend time in the sun to reduce depressive thoughts and boost your mood.

Chapter 3
Tools for Channeling and Transforming Your Grief

> **Embrace each challenge in your life as an opportunity for self-transformation.**
>
> —Bernie Siegel

You have the capacity to transform your grief into greater love and compassion. Right now, it may feel like you are stuck inside a dark tunnel with no glimmer of light anywhere. But trust me, things will get better. At this point, you may find that impossible to believe, but don't forget that all wounds heal. Yes, there will always be a vacuum in your life that was created by the departure of your loved one. But you can fill that void with gratitude and beautiful memories of that person.

You may wonder why you are still here—life may feel purposeless for now. But if you are here, then there's a reason for it. You have work left to do in this world—more purpose that you must fulfill. Besides, the end of your loved one's life does not imply an end of love for you. That wonderful soul whom you loved so much may not be around anymore, but the love in your heart is still there with you. No one can take that love away from you; it is all yours. It doesn't depend on the entry or departure of another soul in your life. They may serve as catalysts for bringing that love to the surface, but the love is still within you—it hasn't gone anywhere, and it is never going to go anywhere.

I hope that makes you feel a little better. I'm not giving you a shallow pep talk. Over time, you will realize the depth and truth of my words. For now, I want to empower you with more tools that you can use to channel and transform your grief. So let's get to it!

Special Release Meditation

This is a very powerful practice. It involves releasing your soul ties with your loved one. A lot of people are resistant to the idea of letting go. They feel that releasing their attachment to their departed loved one implies giving up on that person. That's far from the truth. Releasing your soul ties with your loved one is more about freeing yourself from the bondage of attachment that is causing you so much pain and heartache.

Right now, your attachment to your loved one is causing you pain and suffering. By releasing your attachment to them, you can let go of these negative emotions. The love you shared with them will always be there in your heart. In fact, it will become a lot more accessible once you have removed the shackles of grief and pain.

The Meditation

If you want to first read through this meditation to familiarize yourself with what you'll be doing and then come back to it later on when you are completely ready, that's perfectly fine. Also, if you want, you can record the meditation in your own voice and play it while doing the meditation.

You can also simply take this book with you and read the instructions while doing the meditation. Just make sure that you do so in a quiet and peaceful place where you won't be disturbed. Try to make the space as calming as possible so that it's easy for you to relax completely.

I would also recommend that you keep some handkerchiefs and water around. Since this is a release meditation, you'll have a lot of emotions come up. You may also want to use a blanket to keep yourself warm and comfortable.

When you are ready, lie down or sit comfortably, keeping your spine straight. Close your eyes and start taking a few deep breaths. Place one hand on your stomach and another on your chest; observe how your stomach and chest expand with each inhalation, and with each exhalation, they contract. Continue taking these deep breaths with your eyes closed for the next three to four minutes. Focus your mind completely on your breath. Observe how each breath is entering through your nostrils and expanding through your entire body. If your mind begins to wander, then gently bring it back to the present moment, observing each inhalation and exhalation.

Once you have entered a space of deep relaxation, observe your body to see if there is any pent-up tension or stress anywhere. If any body part has accumulated tension, then fix your focus there. Now, contract that body part and, as you release the contraction, say to yourself, "My (name of body part) is fully relaxed. My whole body is now fully relaxed. I am fully relaxed."

Do this exercise for any and all body parts where you have accumulated tension. Once you have released tension from your body and you're feeling relaxed, visualize a beautiful garden. It is springtime and there are colorful flowers blooming everywhere. You are sitting under the cool shade of a large tree. There is a small oasis near you and on top of it, there is a wooden bridge. On the other side of the bridge, you can see someone walking toward you. You are beside yourself with joy—indeed, it is your loved one!

You are so excited to see them that you run across the bridge to meet them halfway. They are just as delighted to see you as you are. As you are facing them, look into their eyes and allow yourself to feel all the emotions that are coming up. If you want to hug or kiss them, then do it.

Now, tell them whatever it is that you want to say to them. When you have finished, stand in silence to hear if they have anything to say. Once you feel you have said everything you have to say and heard everything you wanted to hear from them, it is time to release them from this attachment. Tell them how grateful you are for all the wonderful times you got to spend together, but now you must let them go as they are no longer on the same physical plane as you. You'll always love them and you know how much they love you.

With the conviction that this love is going to be with you forever, imagine that there are large cords between your belly and theirs. Visualize a giant pair of scissors cutting these cords. You are now free from them and they are free from you. As the connections are cut, your loved one starts moving away from you until they are fully dissolved in the ether.

Even though their physical body is gone, their love and memories will always live in your heart. You are now free from the bondage of your attachment to them. After all, love and attachment are two different things. You don't have to be attached to be someone in order to love them. Real love is an experience of complete and immense freedom in every way possible. Allow yourself to feel this love and gratitude in your heart. Thank the universe, God, or whatever higher power you believe in for having brought such a beautiful soul into your life. Express your gratitude for all the love you have experienced and the good times you have had. Also, express your gratitude for all the love you are going to experience and all the good times you are going to have from now on.

When you are ready, slowly move your fingers and your toes. Bring your palms together and rub them to generate some heat. Place them on your eyelids and then gently open your eyes as you remove them.

Note: This is an extremely powerful meditation. You may think that it's all your imagination, but it's not. We are spiritual beings having a brief human experience. According to the law of thermodynamics, energy can only be transformed—it cannot be created or destroyed. Even though your loved one isn't present with you in their physical body, their energetic presence still exists in this universe. Through this meditation, you are connecting with that energetic presence. If you are really listening, you may even hear startling things from them while you are holding a conversation with them.

A word of caution here: Doing this meditation just once is good enough to release your attachment to your departed loved one. You will definitely feel a shift if you have done the release properly. For some people, it may be necessary to do this meditation several times. I advise against doing this more than twice a month, and ensure at least a period of fourteen days between sessions. The reason is that if done too frequently, this meditation can become a way of continuing to feed your attachment to the departed soul as you are constantly trying to connect with them even though you try and convince yourself it would be the very last time. You cannot bring them back physically. Hence, continuing to feed your attachment will only make you more miserable. To be happy again, you must let go of your attachment.

Meditation for Self-Healing

Unlike the previous meditation, this one can be done every day. In fact, I would strongly recommend that you practice it every day. The two best times for meditation are in the morning immediately after waking up and at night before going to sleep. Of course, you can use this meditation any other time of the day as well. It's just that you will get the maximum benefits out of it if you can practice it twice a day (or at least once a day) at these two times when the doorways of the subconscious mind are wide open.

The subconscious mind carries our deepest beliefs, ideas, and traumas that shape our experience of life. By impacting and reprogramming the subconscious, you can heal yourself and your life. The subconscious is most accessible when we are in a deeply relaxed state that is akin to sleep. Indeed, you can induce such a state at will any time of the day. It's just that all of us experience it right after waking up in the morning and immediately before going to bed at night.

I would strongly recommend that you record the meditation in your own voice to follow along when you are practicing. Alternatively, you can also memorize the steps and replay them from memory. This meditation is less effective when reading as you go.

The Meditation

Find a peaceful place where you won't be disturbed. Sit comfortably, keeping your spine straight. I would strongly recommend that you do this meditation sitting up. The goal is to enter a state of deep relaxation while staying fully awake. It is harder to stay awake when meditating while lying down, but there are also other spiritual reasons for doing this meditation in a sitting position. For example, sitting up aids the circulation of energy.

When you are ready, close your eyes and start taking a few deep breaths. Place one hand on your stomach and another one on your chest; observe how your stomach and chest expand and contract with each inhalation and exhalation.

Continue taking these deep breaths with your eyes closed for the next three to four minutes. Focus your mind completely on your breath. Observe how each breath is entering through your nostrils and expanding through your entire body. If your mind begins to wander, gently bring it back to the present moment, observing each inhalation and exhalation.

Once you have entered a space of deep relaxation, observe your body to see if there is any pent-up tension or stress anywhere. If any body part has accumulated tension, then fix your focus there. Contract that body part and as you release the contraction, say to yourself, "My (name of body part) is fully relaxed. My whole body is now fully relaxed. I am fully relaxed." Do this exercise for any and all body parts where you have accumulated tension.

Now, visualize a small ball of pink light at the center of your heart. This luminous ball represents the unconditional love in your heart. This love that is within you is also present everywhere in the universe. It is the fabric of the universe that holds everything together. As you are continuing to take deep breaths and focusing on this pink ball of light, it is expanding and growing in size.

Now, this pink light encompasses your entire body. There's a soothing energy flowing through your body as you are feeling the vibrations of this pink ball of light. It is like the gentle flow of water. Your body, mind, and soul are being purified by the pink ball of light. If you are feeling pain or discomfort in any particular organ or body part, visualize that area being washed by the soothing water-like energy of this pink ball. Your entire body is now bathed in the energy of unconditional love. All your organs have been healed. You are now full of joy, vitality, and positivity.

Visualize that this ball of light is expanding to encompass the entire room that you are in. It is slowly expanding to encompass your entire neighborhood. The pink ball of energy is growing bigger and bigger—it now encompasses your entire city, your entire country. It is expanding further and further. Now, it covers the entire globe. It is expanding more and more. Now, the entire universe is encompassed within this pink ball of energy. You, your loved ones, everything you have, and everything you desire is encompassed within this pink ball of energy. You are one with the unconditional love of the universe.

If there is any particular situation, body part, or health issue (for you or for someone you love) that needs healing, then visualize that it is getting filled, washed, and soothed by the energy of this pink ball of light. Visualize the outcome that you want and see the pink ball of light encompassing it. Trust that what you wanted to heal has now been fully healed.

If there is anything that you want to manifest, then visualize your desired outcome on the screen of your mind. Allow yourself to feel all the emotions that you'll feel when your wish has been fulfilled. In your mind's eye, see yourself living that moment with joy and rapture.

Visualize that situation being filled by the energy of the pink ball of light. Revel in that moment—rest in the peace and joy of that moment.

When you are ready, slowly move your fingers and toes. Bring your palms together and rub them to generate some heat. Place them on your eyelids and then gently open your eyes as you remove them.

Practicing Affirmations

Affirmations can be another powerful tool to use while rebuilding your life. Affirmations are positive statements that you constantly repeat in your mind or out aloud. Through repetition over time, they create strong impressions on your mind. This is a highly effective method for reprogramming your subconscious and changing your life.

You don't need any special place or time for practicing affirmations. You can do them anytime, anywhere. Although repeating them right after your morning and evening meditations can further enhance the benefits you get from the meditations alone.

Go through the affirmations listed below and pick a few that truly resonate with you. Don't try to do all of them, as that would defy the purpose. Affirmations gain their power through repetition. If you try practicing too many at a given time, you won't be able to pour focused energy into any of them. Hence, pick just one or a few (not more than three) to begin with. Feel free to modify or rewrite them to suit your personal taste. The most important thing is that it should speak to your heart. As you repeat the affirmation, you should feel something mentally and emotionally. Without feeling, affirmations don't have that much power.

Affirmations

- I am healthy, happy, and joyful. Everything is perfect in my life and my world.

- I love myself. Everyone around me loves me. I am deeply loved and I love deeply. All is well in my world.

- I have everything that I desire and need. I am deeply content and fulfilled. I am where I wish and need to be at this moment in time.

- Today is a perfect day. Everything is happening according to God's/the universe's perfect plan. I know I can relax and trust God/the universe perfectly.

- With every moment, I am renewing and recreating myself. Right now, I am exactly who I wish and want to be. I am grateful for what I have, who I am, and who I have in my life. All is well in my world.

- My heart is completely at peace. It is filled with unconditional love.

- It is easy for me to give and receive love because love is the essence of my being.

- I choose to be happy, peaceful, and content today.

- It is easy for me to love and accept myself exactly the way I am. I accept and love myself unconditionally.

- Today is a perfect day to be healthy, happy, and loving. I am a very healthy, happy, and loving person.

Practicing Gratitude

Gratitude is the most powerful form of prayer you can practice. We can become so lost in our grief that we forget to be thankful for everything and everyone that we still have in our lives. By simply making a habit out of practicing gratitude on a daily basis, you will make significant progress on your healing journey.

So how do you start practicing gratitude? Here are a few tips that you can incorporate into your daily life:

Start a gratitude journal: Every morning right after you open your eyes, start your day with gratitude. Write down three things you are grateful for that day. Do this same practice before retiring to bed, except that at night, write down three things that happened on that day that you are truly grateful for. Again, this doesn't have to be anything big. It can be something small or that you would otherwise consider to be insignificant. This practice is all about compelling us to recognize how blessed we truly are. If you don't want to do this twice a day (though I would strongly recommend that you do), then stick to doing just the morning practice.

Every day, challenge yourself to come up with something new. This will compel you to think about the things you might be taking for granted. You don't have to come up with the big things every time. Both the big and small things are equally important in the grand scheme of things. Something as simple as "I'm grateful for the pen I am writing with," is just as powerful as "I am grateful to have a beautiful loving family."

Starting your day with gratitude will help you set the right precedent for the rest of your day. Don't skip this practice on those days when you are really feeling blue. Those are the days when you need to practice gratitude more than ever. There's always so much that is going well in life. When you start looking, you'll realize you are more blessed than you thought—there's really a lot to be grateful for. Unfortunately, as humans, we have a tendency to take things for granted. We don't realize the value of what we have until we lose it. You don't want to live like that. So always start and end your days with gratitude!

Practice gratitude whenever you are feeling negative: Gratitude is an alchemical process that can instantly transform pain and grief into love and appreciation. Whenever you are feeling negative or pessimistic, shift your focus to what is going well in your life and all that you are grateful for.

Thank others often: A lot of the time, we take other people's efforts at making our life more convenient and beautiful for granted. Get in the habit of saying thank you for even the smallest acts of kindness you receive from others. And I am not talking about saying thank you to just your near and dear ones, but also to that shop assistant who helped you out with patience and attention, or the bus driver who helped you get to your destination.

I am talking about developing an attitude and habit of thankfulness. By simply saying a thank you with a smile, you can make other people's days more beautiful. It doesn't cost you anything, but it enriches your life and the lives of others.

Explore an Interest or Passion

We all have a list of things we wish we had done. A lot of times we think it's too late now to try our hands at it. Trust me, it is never too late to try something new and maybe even become good at it. So now is really the perfect time to sign up for those adult ballet classes or start riding a motorcycle.

By focusing on a new hobby, you'll be able to channel the energy of grief into constructive, creative energy. When you are grieving, there is nothing worse than just sitting around and constantly replaying in your mind what has already transpired. Instead, get up and get going. Let the passing of your loved one be a reminder about the temporal nature of life. No one knows how much time they have left for living in this world. Hence, you must spend every day as if it were going to be your last because one day, you are going to be right!

Chapter Summary

- The end of your loved one's life does not imply an end of love for you. The love in your heart is still there. No one can take that love away—it hasn't gone anywhere and it is never going to go anywhere.

- People feel that releasing their attachment with their departed loved one implies giving up on that person, but that's far from the truth. Releasing your soul ties with your loved one is more about freeing yourself from the bondage of attachment that is causing you so much pain and heartache.

- The two best times for meditation are in the morning immediately after waking up and at night before going to sleep.

- Don't do the release meditation more than twice a month and ensure at least a period of fourteen days between sessions.

- The subconscious mind carries our deepest beliefs, ideas, and traumas that shape our experience of life. By impacting and reprogramming the subconscious, you can heal yourself and your life.

- Affirmations are positive statements that you constantly repeat in your mind or out aloud. Through repetition over time, they create strong impressions and your mind. This is a highly effective method for reprogramming your subconscious and changing your life.

- You can do affirmations anytime, anywhere. Although repeating them right after your morning and evening meditations can further enhance the benefits you get from meditation.

- Start with only a few affirmations. When choosing affirmations, keep in mind how they feel in your heart. You should feel something mentally and emotionally when repeating them; without feeling, affirmations don't have much power.

- Gratitude is the most powerful form of prayer you can ever practice. By simply making a habit of practicing gratitude on a daily basis, you will make significant progress on your healing journey.

- Every morning after you open your eyes, start your day with gratitude. Write down three things you are grateful for that day. Do this same practice before retiring to bed, writing down three things that happened on that day that you are grateful for.

- Whenever you are feeling negative or pessimistic, shift your focus to what is going well in your life and all that you are grateful for.

- Get in the habit of saying thank you for even the smallest acts of kindness you receive from others.

- Try focusing on a new hobby. By doing so, you'll be able to channel the energy of grief into constructive and creative energy.

Chapter 4
Understanding the Different Grieving Styles and How to Help Someone Who Is Grieving

> Grief can't be shared. Everyone carries it alone. His own burden in his own way.
>
> —Anne Morrow Lindbergh

When a person dies, everyone who was close to that individual is affected in some way. Roles and responsibilities shift as people adapt to a new reality without the loved one. Since people have different individual personalities, there are significant differences in how each individual experiences, expresses, and handles grief. Just because another person in your family isn't reacting to the loss in the same manner as you are doesn't mean they aren't grieving in their own way.

Researchers have identified three primary styles of grieving.³ In most cases, the grieving individual identifies much more strongly with one of these styles versus the other two. But they can also be a combination of two different styles. Keep in mind that these styles of grieving are broad spectrums and not strict categories. People don't just grieve in different ways, they also experience grief differently at different times and at varying levels of intensity.

Understanding these different grieving styles will help you develop a better understanding of your own grieving style while also developing a greater empathy for how your near and dear ones are coping as well.

Instrumental grievers: People who are instrumental grievers experience and talk about their grief in intellectual, physical, and cognitive terms. Someone who experiences grief in this manner likely has a personality that's more action oriented. If you ask them how they are feeling in the face of this life-altering loss, they may respond by sharing what they have done or are doing. For instance, they may tell you how they immediately started taking steps to further their loved one's legacy, or how they contributed to a charity in honor of them.

Someone with an instrumental grieving style is generally most comfortable with analyzing facts and making informed decisions to solve problems. On the surface, they appear strong, detached, and dispassionate even in the face of a life-altering loss.

Since they talk in such a rational and intellectual way about their loss, others may misinterpret their response as being cold or uncaring. However, that's not the truth at all. They are just experiencing and expressing strong emotions in a very different way.

Intuitive grievers: People who are intuitive grievers are strongly attuned to their feelings. They are also highly sensitive to the feelings of others. They express their emotions in terms of feelings. They might say, "I have been so sad and devastated that I struggle to get out of bed every

---

[3] "Understanding Different Bereavement Styles in Your Family." *In Touch Bereavement Newsletter*. July/August 2017. Bereavement Department, hov.org. Accessed November 13, 2021. https://hov.org/media/1765/bit-jul-aug-2017.pdf.

morning," "I cry myself to sleep every night," or "At times, I feel maddening rage toward everyone. Why me?" As you can see, their response to grief is all about exploring and expressing the wide array of emotions they are going through.

These individuals are comfortable with experiencing such strong emotions. They don't try to hold back their tears or put on a brave face. Due to their emotional and sensitive nature, it is very difficult for them to intellectualize or rationalize their pain. They may appear completely overwhelmed and totally devastated by the loss—that might be the truth anyway.

Dissonant grievers: People who are dissonant grievers experience a massive conflict between their internal experience of grief and how they externally express it. This conflict, or dissonance, can be due to cultural, social, or family expectations or norms. Such an individual may be internally experiencing a tsunami of emotions, but they struggle to hide it as they must preserve the image that they are projecting to the world. On the opposite end of the spectrum, another individual may feel terribly guilty for not feeling the kind of strong overwhelming emotions that others are expecting them to.

Gender Differences in Grieving Styles

It is important to understand that neither all men nor all women grieve in a style that is stereotypically associated with their gender. In general, men are associated more strongly with the instrumental grieving style, while it is more common for women to grieve in the intuitive style.

But we must be careful not to generalize this to the extent that we start believing that all women grieve in the intuitive style and all men in the instrumental style. Despite the generalization being true for a large percentage of men, there are many who grieve in the intuitive style just as there is a large percentage of women who grieve in a more instrumental style.

Grieving styles depend a lot more upon an individual's personality than on their gender. When we fail to take into consideration these fundamental differences in personality, we compel a person to experience dissonant grief. Allow yourself and others to grieve in the way that comes naturally to you and to them.

That being said, it is quite common for men to throw themselves into time-bound tasks in the face of loss. For instance, a man may preoccupy himself with planning a perfect funeral for his deceased wife, or he may start spending most of his time taking on additional responsibilities at work. These activities give the man a reason to keep going, while also serving as a means for escaping his grief.

Men are also more likely to cry when they are alone. They usually don't publicly show their emotions or allow themselves to appear vulnerable when others are around. It is also likely that they may avoid having conversations about the deceased loved one, as that can bring up uncomfortable emotions which they may not want to deal with.

Women, on the other hand, are usually intuitive grievers. They are likely to be more open with their feelings and they also generally feel a strong need to share with others what they are thinking and feeling. So a woman would feel better around someone who is comfortable with strong emotions and is willing to listen to what she has to say without passing any judgment.

Now, I don't want you to start judging and badgering yourself if you aren't experiencing grief in the way that is considered more stereotypical for your gender. There is nothing wrong with you. You must always remember that having a more instrumental grieving style while being a woman doesn't make you any less of a woman. Similarly, having a more intuitive grieving style doesn't make you any less of a man.

When my sister died, everyone expected me to cry hysterically when her body was being taken away from the hospital room. To my and everyone else's surprise, I didn't shed a tear. But that didn't mean I wasn't crying on the inside. I have always noticed how I manage to remain rational and relatively calm even in the face of extremely challenging circumstances. This experience taught me a lot about myself, as I realized even though I am very traditionally feminine in so many ways, my response to grief is usually more instrumental. There were also times when I broke down completely and couldn't hold back my tears in front of others. So I won't box myself completely in one category alone. As human beings, our emotions and thoughts are extremely complex. Any kind of categorization can serve as a general guide to help us understand ourselves and others better, but it's not wise to adhere to it fanatically.

We must also remain empathetic to ourselves and to others. I know this is not easy when we are all fighting our own inner battles. If you are an instrumental griever and your partner is an intuitive griever, you may struggle to figure out how best you can support them. In the same way, you may feel alone and lost when your grieving style is intuitive, but your partner is experiencing their grief in a more instrumental fashion. In this chapter, I'll give you some practical tips on how you can be there for your loved ones in a supportive way as they are dealing with their own grief and also how you can ask them for support as you are undergoing your own turmoil.

How Children Grieve

Children grieve just as deeply as adults do. However, depending upon the level of their cognitive and emotional development, children may experience and express it differently than the adults around them. I would not recommend trying to shield the child from the reality of the situation by providing false hope or giving inauthentic information.

Children should be given accurate and factual information along with the freedom to ask whatever questions may arise in their minds. Let them express their feelings and listen to any input they may want to offer during family discussions. Treating a child with respect is very important. Your child may be small, but they are still an autonomous individual with complex emotions and a unique way of thinking. Don't minimize the gravity of what they are facing and going through.

The Dos and Don'ts of Helping a Child Grieve

Here are some pointers to keep in mind when you are helping a child grieve.

Do:

- Convey the truth about what has happened. The amount of details you provide depends upon the child's age and their cognitive abilities.
- Allow the child to attend the funeral, even if the child is very young.
- Try to keep the child's daily routine as normal as possible.
- Listen to your child attentively and with respect when they want to share their feelings with you.
- Check in with your child to see how they are doing. Don't force them to talk if they aren't ready for it.
- Help your child find ways to honor, memorialize, and symbolize the deceased person.
- Get your child to engage in creative activity like drawing or writing. This might help them release pent-up emotions.
- Pay attention to how your child is playing, especially when alone. They may be communicating and channeling their grief through games.

Don't:

- Force the child to mourn publicly if they aren't comfortable with it.
- Give false hope or deliver confusing messages like "Grandpa is asleep," or "Grandma has gone on vacation."

- Tell the child to stay quiet or to stop crying in order to not upset others.

- Try to shield the child from the truth of the situation. Children are far more intuitive and intelligent than people realize. Let your child face the reality of the situation.

- Pretend that everything is normal. It is okay to let yourself cry in front of your child. This sends the message that it's okay to cry and may help your child express their own feelings.

- Rely on the child for emotional support. It is one thing to let your tears show and another to start relying on a small child for emotional support. It is okay to share your feelings with your child, but don't treat them as your personal confidant—only an adult should be your confidant.

Ways In Which You Can Support a Grieving Family Member or Friend

It is very difficult to watch someone you love grappling with pain and grief. You really want to help them feel better, but it may seem very hard to understand what you should or shouldn't do. The situation becomes all the more challenging when you are also handling your own grief and the other person has a completely different grieving style than you.

I know how hard this is because I have been there myself. I was afraid of saying the wrong thing—of making their pain worse by inadvertently doing something that could rub them the wrong way. What I learned was that my efforts to be there for my grieving loved ones were never in vain. The most important thing you can do during a difficult time is simply be there. You don't have to know the right answers or have the perfect advice to offer. Your loving presence and unconditional support is what they need at this difficult hour.

Not reaching out for fear of doing something wrong would be the biggest mistake. Here are some tips that can help you understand how you can support your grieving loved one.

Respect Their Grieving Style

A lot of times we try to be helpful by telling someone what they should be thinking, feeling, or doing. Even though such behavior stems out of a genuine desire to help, you must avoid offering that kind of advice at all costs. Give them enough space to grieve in their own way.

After all, there is no right or wrong way to grieve. Grief is, in itself, a very complex state to undergo that brings a wide array of complex emotions to the surface. The last thing you want to do is make matters worse for them by making them feel they aren't doing something right.

Just Be There

You don't want to offer help in a way that feels right to you. You want to offer help in the way that best supports your grieving loved one. We often try to give another person what we would like for ourselves if we were in their situation. But what you need might be completely different from what your loved one needs.

It is best to just be there for them—and by this I mean being fully present, eliminating all distractions. Give them 100 percent of your attention and truly listen when they tell you something. Let them also know that you are there for them in whatever way they desire. Tell them that you are eager to help and you would do anything to ease their pain. You just need their help in understanding what you can do for them.

Now, don't expect to get a straightforward answer. Many people just don't know what they want but you'll find enough cues in their behavior. For instance, if your loved one keeps crying and saying,

"Why me?" repeatedly, they may be seeking some comforting words from you. In case you really don't know what you should be saying or doing, just be there—hold their hand, hug them, comfort them in your arms. Such gestures speak louder than words ever can! And when your loved one wants to talk, listen to them keenly.

Speak kind and empathetic words. Never say anything that negates or devalues their feelings. This can happen when one person has an instrumental grieving style and the other grieves in a more intuitive style. The person with the instrumental style might intellectualize the situation too much, making the intuitive person feel like their emotions are not valued.

The person with the intuitive grieving style must also be careful not to accuse the person with the instrumental style of being unemotional or unaffected by the situation. To make them feel valued, appreciate the work they are doing at this difficult time.

Ease Their Burden

Ask them if there is anything specific you can help them out with right now. If they don't offer any suggestions right away, you can make a few offers from your side. For instance, you can offer to cook dinner or give them a lift for important errands. Try to assess which area they are most struggling with, and then make an offer accordingly. Just make sure that you are truly comfortable with the offer that you are making. Don't offer to do something if there is even the minutest possibility that you'll feel resentful about following through on your commitments.

Also, don't make vague offers like "Let me do something for you." Tell them exactly what you would like to do for them. Here are some ideas for the different ways in which you can help:

- Run errands on their behalf
- Cook for them
- Do the laundry
- Clean their house
- Help with childcare responsibilities
- Take care of any dependents they may have
- Manage and coordinate bills
- Help with paperwork

- Financial help (if you can)

Practice Patience

There are usually a lot of things that need to be taken care of within the initial days and weeks after a death. Your grieving loved one would likely appreciate having your support with getting things done. You'll have to be extra patient as they will be feeling very vulnerable and raw adjusting to this new reality. They may suffer from emotional outbursts and crying spells every now and then. It's possible that they may also get very angry at times. Try your best to not take it personally as it likely has nothing to do with you.

The other most important thing you should keep in mind is the fact that there is no timeline for grieving. Your loved one may be able to get back to a semblance of normalcy within a few weeks or they may need your support for months or even years. Be sure to make a note of special days to get in touch with them. Those may be some of the toughest days in the year for them.

Get Them Engaged in an Activity

Weekends or holidays may be very difficult for your loved one, as they might struggle with loneliness. Suggest doing an activity together that you both enjoy. If your loved one is comfortable and wants to reminisce about the deceased individual, then you can even plan to go through old photographs or videos together. Just make sure that the activity you are suggesting is something that you are both comfortable with. Your presence alone can be extremely reassuring and supportive.

Don't Try to Fix Them

This is the biggest mistake that people make. They think that the grieving individual is like a broken clock that needs to be fixed. We've all met that person who tells us to move on and forget the loss. That never feels good.

No one can ever overcome the trauma and pain from a life-altering loss by hearing that kind of advice. In fact, that kind of advice has the opposite effect on people—it can be annoying and irksome. Only the wearer knows where the shoe pinches. If it was that easy to overcome mental and emotional trauma, then everyone in the world would be happy. But it's not—every person in this world is fighting an invisible battle that we know nothing about. We have no right to undermine the enormity of what they are dealing with.

It is really important that you suspend all judgment and just be there for your loved one. Don't be afraid of tears, anger, and emotional outbursts. Don't try to stop them when they are having an explosive moment (as long as they aren't harming themselves or someone else). Accept and validate their grief even if a long time has passed since the death. Your task is to simply be present with your loved one—it's not your job to fix them.

Get Them to Open Up

A lot of times you may feel a desperate desire to help your grieving loved one, but you feel as if there are walls blocking you from getting close to them. The best way to get them to open up is by sharing something personal and relatable. Like, you can tell them you understand what they are going through since you went through something similar when you lost your father, or something like that. People are a lot more likely to share their feelings and thoughts when they have some kind of reassurance that it would be respected and there won't be any judgment.

If you can't think of anything, then just start by asking them if they have been eating on time or getting enough sleep. Slowly, you can venture into asking questions about their mental and emotional state—how they have been feeling, what has been on their mind, and so on. Just make sure that you aren't being nosy or too intrusive. This definitely requires a fine balancing act.

Also, when they do share more details with you, don't be afraid to ask follow-up questions. Most people fear asking questions lest they may upset the grieving individual. When they speak, be sure to listen attentively and compassionately.

If the person is giving monosyllabic answers, then you can simply ask, "Do you feel like talking right now?" If they say no, then just be there with them in silence.

Again, it's not your job to fix them. Grief is a burden that every individual must carry on their own. You can't do it for them. But your presence, love, support, and compassion can still make a world of difference to your loved one.

Make Them Laugh

Don't be afraid to share something funny or silly that can make the grieving individual laugh. Just make sure that you are being sensitive and not saying anything that could hurt their feelings. The safest would be to share something funny that happened with you, or a joke that is completely unrelated to them. This can serve as a positive distraction from their grief and they may be able to experience a few lighthearted moments amid all the tears and sadness.

Give Them a Gift

It is common practice to send flowers to a grieving person. You can do it if you think they'll appreciate the flowers. But I would also encourage you to think outside the box and give them something they would appreciate more, like a thoughtful letter or card, a home-cooked meal, baked goodies, a box of self-care items, memorabilia, and so on. The gift doesn't have to be anything expensive (though it can be if that's what you want and you are sure it would make them happy). What matters most here is the thought behind the gift—by giving them something valuable you are telling them that you care for them and you're there for them.

Don't Be Afraid to Mention the Deceased Person's Name

Many people wrongly assume that mentioning the deceased person's name should be avoided at all costs. Indeed, it can trigger some tears but those triggers were already present and just waiting to come out at the right moment. It feels a lot worse to think that someone who was dearly loved must be expunged permanently from memory and conversation. Mentioning how much you miss the deceased person can come across as being a lot more empathetic than a cursory, "I am sorry for your loss."

Things You Shouldn't Say to a Grieving Person

- **"It's all part of God's plan."** This can really anger people. They may respond with rage saying, "What plan? I don't want to be a part of this plan."

- **"I'm sure they are in a better place now."** The grieving person may really struggle with believing this. It is best to keep such beliefs to yourself.

- **"You still have a lot to be thankful for."** They may feel like you are trying to diminish the gravity and magnitude of what they are facing. They already know what they have and don't have in life. This statement can feel like you are forcing them to overlook their grief.

- **"It's time to put everything behind you and move on with life."** You don't know what the other person is really dealing with. Grief is such a complex experience. Every individual's experience with it is bound to be unique and different. People move on when they are ready to do so and not when they are told they should.

- **"How are you."** The answer is obviously "not good." Also, since this is a generic greeting, it doesn't acknowledge the loss and the pain that the other person is going through. Instead, try saying: "How are you feeling?" or "Would you like to talk?"

- **Abstain from *should*s, *will*s, and *must*s.** Using these words can make it seem like you are giving the other person a command. It is a lot more compassionate to say something like, "Have you thought about . . .?" "Would you like to try . . ." or "Have you considered . . .?"

Chapter Summary

- Just because another person in your family isn't reacting to the loss in the same manner as you doesn't mean they aren't grieving in their own way.

- Instrumental grievers experience and talk about their grief in intellectual, physical, and cognitive terms.

- Intuitive grievers are strongly attuned to their feelings. They are also highly sensitive to other people's feelings. They express their emotions in terms of feelings.

- Dissonant grievers experience a massive conflict between their internal experience of grief and how they are externally expressing it. This conflict or dissonance can be due to cultural, social or family expectations/norms.

- In general, men are associated more strongly with the instrumental grieving style and women with the intuitive style. But we must be careful not to generalize this to the extreme. Grieving styles depend a lot more upon an individual's personality than on their gender. Allow yourself and others to grieve in the way that comes naturally to you and to them.

- Children grieve just as deeply as adults do. However, depending upon the level of their cognitive and emotional development, children may experience and express it differently than the adults around them.

- Children should be given accurate and factual information, along with the freedom to ask whatever questions may arise in their minds. Let them express their feelings and listen to any input they may want to offer during family discussions.

- When helping someone you love cope with grief, remember to give them all of your attention and truly listen when they tell you something. Tell them that you are eager to help and you would do anything to ease their pain. You just need their help in understanding what you can do for them.

- The best way to get someone to open up is by sharing something personal and relatable. Don't be afraid to share something funny or silly that can make the grieving individual laugh. Just make sure that you are being sensitive and not saying anything that can hurt their feelings.

- It feels a lot worse to think that someone who was dearly loved must be expunged permanently from memory and conversation. Mentioning how much you miss the deceased person can come across as being a lot more empathetic than a cursory, "I am sorry for your loss."

Chapter 5
How to Ask for Help and the Art of Receiving

> **Asking for help is never a sign of weakness. It's one of the bravest things you can do.**
>
> **And it can save your life.**
>
> —Lily Collins, *Unfiltered: No Shame, No Regrets, Just Me*

For most of us, asking for help is undoubtedly the most difficult thing we can ever do. We are afraid that asking for help will make us appear weak and incompetent in other people's eyes. That's far from the truth.

Most of the time, people don't know what's on our mind or what we are going through—this is true even for the people closest to us. Our loved ones would really like to be there for us and help us in whatever way we need. The problem is, they don't really know what you need unless you tell them. Of course, this requires one to put their ego aside and face the possibility of your request being denied. But the thing is, if you don't try, you definitely won't get what you need. The chances of the other person figuring out exactly what you need on their own are always slim to none.

Don't be afraid that people will judge you just because you are asking for help. People are generally quite happy to do things for their loved ones, as it gives them a chance to shown how much they care; they gain an opportunity to express their love. Asking for and accepting help from others is an important life skill that everyone should learn and master. There is no such thing as a completely self-made person. We constantly need the love and support of others to thrive in our own lives.

There is nothing shameful about asking for help. In fact, it takes great courage and strength to put ego aside and admit that you need help. Of course, it also requires you to assume a position of vulnerability. Being vulnerable is not the same as being weak. I really believe that only a strong person can be vulnerable, because they are willing to let others see their true self—irrespective of outcome.

Why Is Asking for Help So Hard?

Fear of rejection is the biggest reason why we refrain from asking for help. There is also an element of relinquishing control involved, which is a very fearful prospect for many people. Fear often overrides our ability to reason. Also, it is important to note that the risk of experiencing emotional pain can activate the same regions of the brain as physical pain.

Another important reason why many people struggle with asking for help is because they just don't know how to articulate their needs. Social psychologists call it the *illusion of transparency*—"a tendency for people to overestimate the degree to which their personal mental state is known by others."[4]

---

[4] "The Illusion of Transparency: Why You're Not as Obvious as You Think You Are." Effectiviology. n.d. Accessed November 13, 2021. https://effectiviology.com/illusion-of-transparency/.

We often expect others to read our minds to know what we are thinking and feeling. We want to get our needs met without having to utter a word. Of course, things don't work like that. No matter how close someone is to you, they can't always figure out what you are thinking or feeling. They are likely quite puzzled and clueless about how to meet your needs if you aren't providing any guidance.

If you are always making telepathic pleas for help that no one answers, then it is time to work a bit on your communication style. The best way to get the help you need is by asking for what you want—verbally and clearly. Let go of your inhibitions and ego; asking for help isn't going to diminish your worth. The people who really care about you will appreciate receiving the guidance to know exactly what they can do for you. So here are some tips on how to ask for help:

1. **Be clear, concise, and specific:** You have to know exactly what you want and then ask for it in a clear and concise way. Be as specific as you can so that there is no room for misinterpretation or misunderstanding. You don't need to overexplain. Just make it clear what the task is, why it matters to you, how it will help you, and exactly what the person can do for you.

When you are specific with your request, the other person is better able to assess what kind of time, energy, or other resources it would take to meet your needs. Stay open to possibilities and be willing to negotiate. Let them decide how much help and support they can offer you. Always do your best to find mutually beneficial solutions.

Here are a few pointers to consider when you are trying to make a clear, concise, and specific request:

What: Exactly what is it that you need? Put all ego and hesitation aside and state your need in plain, simple language.

Who: Who needs the help? Do you need help for yourself, or for someone else? Do you need them to help you and someone else or others together?

How: Exactly how can they help you?

Why: Why are you asking them for help—do they have any specific skills, knowledge, or ability that can help successfully complete the task?

Where: Exactly where do you need the help? Specify the areas where you need their assistance. If you need help in a specific physical location, then let them know.

When: When do you need help—is it on a specific day or at a specific time? Is there a deadline for completing the task?

2. **Don't apologize:** Have you ever had that experience where someone asked you for help and then they kept apologizing incessantly? "I'm so sorry about asking you to do this favor," "I feel terrible about having to bother you so much," "I really wish I didn't have to bug you right now," "I know how busy you are—I should really be able to do this myself," "I absolutely hate myself for asking you to help with this," "I'm feeling awful—I must have ruined your plans for the evening."

Receiving a request wrapped in so many apologies doesn't feel good. Be honest with yourself: Have you been guilty of this? Most of us would answer yes. Apologizing while asking for help creates a feeling that you and the other person aren't on the same team. After all, you wouldn't apologize so much if you felt that helping each other was part of the group camaraderie—something that the other person actually wants to do.

Apologizing profusely doesn't help anyone and it certainly doesn't improve your relationship with the other person. It creates a negative dynamic that leaves both parties feeling somewhat unhappy and annoyed. Instead, you should focus on offering praise and appreciation for the other person's help. This will make them feel that their help is truly valued and cherished.

3. **Don't use disclaimers:** This ties in with a previous point. Don't use disclaimers like, "I'm really not the type who asks for help," "I'm asking you only because I have no other choice at this point," or "I wouldn't ask you if I had another choice." When you are trying too hard to prove you are not greedy or weak, it adds a

negative dimension to the conversation. Instead, focus on offering appreciation. Genuine, heartfelt appreciation also increases the chances of getting requests answered favorably.

4. **Don't try to sell the idea to the other person by emphasizing how they'll love it:** We all hate being sold to, and when a person starts saying how much we'll love helping them, it starts sounding like a sales pitch. So, for instance, don't say anything like, "I was wondering if you could take me there next week? It would be a great road trip for you." Just ask nicely—they'll accept if they can. Trying to show them the benefits of helping you isn't going to increase your likelihood of receiving what you want. Instead, it is a lot more likely that you'll end up annoying the other person.

5. **Don't try to portray the help you need as a small or insignificant favor:** Since asking for help is not easy, we often try to portray what we need as something small. For instance, you might find yourself saying something like this: "Would you mind picking up the file from Rob's place? It's practically on your way home," or "Can you put these groceries in the refrigerator? I don't think it will take more than two minutes."

6. Portraying the help you need as something insignificant or small also diminishes the effort that the other person would put in to meet your request. This prevents any warmth from developing as a result of one person's generosity and the other person's gracious acceptance of it.

7. **Don't try to make the other person feel like they owe you something:** Again, since asking for help is so uncomfortable for many of us, we might try to claim the help we want as something that's our right. Even if you have actually done the person a favor in the past, don't mention it. It is highly likely that they remember it themselves. Reminding them of it may make them feel obligated; thus, increasing your chances of receiving a yes, but it won't be a genuine, heartfelt gesture on their part. Besides, if you really have to remind someone of a favor you did for them,

they probably don't see that favor in the same light you do. It also feels like you are keeping a scorecard, and no one likes that!

8. **Avoid asking for help over text or email:** Researchers have found that face-to-face requests are a lot more likely to receive a favorable response than requests made over text or email.[5] It is easier to refuse requests made over text or email since we aren't looking at the other person. So, we don't have to really think about how our decision affects the other person. Even if someone doesn't set out with the intention to respond positively and affirmatively to your request, you can still expect them to change their mind while they are in your presence. This is because people change their minds all the time based on the situation and the people around them. Being able to look at the other person while making a decision can strongly influence the outcome. Of course, there can be situations where asking in person is simply impossible. In that case, it would be a better idea to make the request over a phone or video call. Making requests over text or email should be a last resort.

9. **Don't make your request transactional:** It may seem like a good idea to mention how you'll return the favor at a later date, but this can make the relationship seem very transactional. Besides, no one likes the feeling of being indebted to another person. Moreover, throwing in a return favor can give the impression that you think their help has a certain bartering value. Of course, this is not a strict rule by any means. There can be situations or relationships where promising a return favor at a later date may be a good idea. But in general, I don't think it is something you should do regularly. Also, make sure that you are polite with your requests. Always use please and thank you. Be careful that your requests don't sound like demands.

---

[5] M. Mahdi Roghanizad and Vanessa K. Bohns. "Ask in Person: You're Less Persuasive than You Think over Email." *Journal of Experimental Social Psychology* 69. March 2017. 223–226.
https://www.sciencedirect.com/science/article/abs/pii/S002210311630292X.

10. **Be generous in your appreciation:** I know I have repeated this many times, but it is so important that I must include it as a separate point here. Every person's favorite subject is their own self. Just think about it—when you are looking at a picture, who are your eyes searching for? Your own self, right? The same is true for every person in this world. People love hearing good things about themselves. Just make sure that you are genuine with your words. There's a fine line between flattery and appreciation—it mostly depends on your intentions. Make sure that you are specific in your compliments. Don't say generic things like, "You are so generous." Make it personal and specific by stating exactly why you have that perception of them. So you could say something like: "You are so generous. You took time off work to help me move. I just want you to know that I genuinely appreciate it. I wouldn't have been able to do it without you."

11. **Share the results with them:** Apart from expressing gratitude and appreciation, it is also a good idea to follow up with the results of how their efforts benefitted you. Even though generosity is its own reward, all of us desire to feel like we are being effective. It feels really good to know that the help we offered or the work we did really made a difference in someone's life.

Receiving Graciously

In our highly individualistic society, we are conditioned to believe that we should be able to do everything on our own. So it's not surprising then that even when we do manage to ask for help, it is hard receiving it without feeling guilty or indebted. Receiving anything of value from others is even harder when it comes to us unsolicited—when another person wants to do something for us out of the goodness of their heart.

> Until we can receive with an open heart, we're never really giving with an open heart. When we attach judgment to receiving help, we knowingly or unknowingly attach judgment to giving help.
>
> —*Brené Brown, The Gifts of Imperfection*

I feel receiving graciously is an art that we must master. Yes, giving is important but keeping your heart open to receive with gratitude and grace is equally important.

Understanding The Ben Franklin Effect

The Ben Franklin Effect is a very interesting psychological phenomenon that explains how receiving graciously increases our chances of receiving more kindness and generosity from another person. As you can guess, this phenomenon is named after the legendary founding father of the United States, Benjamin Franklin.[6]

In his autobiography, Franklin described this phenomenon as an old maxim: "He that has once done you a kindness will be more ready to do you another, than he whom you yourself have obliged."[7] He also explains how he managed to transform the animosity of a rival legislator using this same phenomenon. Here's what he said in his own words:

> *Having heard that he had in his library a certain very scarce and curious book, I wrote a note to him, expressing my desire of perusing that book, and requesting he would do me the favor of lending it to me for a few days. He sent it immediately, and I returned it in about a week with another note, expressing strongly my sense of the favor. When we next met in the House, he spoke to me (which he had never done before), and with great civility; and he ever after manifested a readiness to serve me on*

---

[6] "Ben Franklin Effect." [Webpage]. Tabroot, July 23, 2020. https://tabroot.com/ben-franklin-effect/.

[7] Benjamin Franklin. *The Autobiography of Benjamin Franklin*. (New York: Pocket Books, 1954).

all occasions, so that we became great friends, and our friendship continued to his death.[8]

In summary, people tend to like us more when they are kind to us. Of course, it goes without saying that you also have to be kind and respectful to others. But the point is that you don't need to make someone indebted in order to increase your chances of receiving a favor from them. In fact, your chances of receiving a favor are much higher if you have already graciously received a favor from another person.

We all want to feel good about ourselves. When a person shows genuine appreciation and gratitude for something we have done for them, it makes us want to act with even greater generosity and kindness toward them the next time we get a chance.

Being open to receiving graciously from others can deepen and strengthen our relationship with them. I know this is completely contrary to what we are generally taught. If someone does something for us, we immediately start feeling obliged to do something in return. Most of the time, a genuine heartfelt thank you, along with honest appreciation and praise, is all they need from us.

Just Say Thank You

A lot of times we don't receive kindness from others because we don't feel worthy of it. For instance, many people are very uncomfortable with compliments. When they hear compliments like, "You are looking very beautiful today," they may respond saying something like, "Oh it's nothing. Maybe it's just my new sweater." Receiving compliments is very hard for most people and it's usually because they have been conditioned from a young age to not have a high opinion of themselves, lest they become arrogant.

This is far from the truth. Having a high opinion of yourself doesn't make you arrogant or self-absorbed. It makes you self-confident and self-reliant. You are not looking for anyone else to make you feel good

---

[8] Benjamin Franklin. *The Autobiography of Benjamin Franklin*. (New York: Pocket Books, 1954).

about yourself. You already know your worth and no one can diminish your opinion of yourself with criticism.

Working to receive compliments graciously is the first step toward opening your heart to receiving kindness from others. Next time someone pays you a compliment, reply with a heartfelt thank you. Don't try to disparage their compliment. You can say something like, "Thank you. You are very kind."

This kind of gracious acceptance of compliments makes both the giver and the receiver feel good. You don't need to immediately pay a compliment in return to the giver. Your compliment would be appreciated more and come across as a lot more genuine if it is given at another time and place and not as a rebuttal to the compliment the other person paid you.

Same goes for receiving any tangible gifts. Next time someone wants to take you to a nice place for lunch, don't reject their gift by saying, "It's too expensive," or something like that. Instead, accept it and then thank them for the wonderful time you had.

Similarly, don't reject other people's offers to make your life easier. Let others share your load and make things lighter for you. Again, all you need to do in return is to offer genuine praise and appreciation. Receive graciously—but always with gratitude and appreciation. The gratitude and appreciation must be there in your heart and they must also be verbally expressed.

Pay It Forward

As I said earlier, don't try to do something in return immediately after receiving a gift (unless, of course, that's what's needed or what feels right to your heart). If you are trying to find something to give to someone just because you are feeling obliged or indebted, you need to stop. You are actually deflecting the love that they have given you. After all, their gift to you is, in essence, an expression of their love and affection for you.

You must wait until the right opportunity comes to give them something. But then, it must come from the heart and shouldn't be a gift that you are giving simply because they have given you something in the past. Also, instead of trying to pay back a gift, try paying forward. Bless someone else with your generosity and kindness just like that person did for you.

Chapter Summary

- Our loved ones would really like to be there for us and help us in whatever way we need. The problem is they don't know what you need unless you tell them.

- There is nothing shameful about asking for help. In fact, it takes great courage and strength to put ego aside and admit that you need help.

- Most people struggle with asking for help because they just don't know how to articulate their needs. Social psychologists call it the illusion of transparency.

- When asking for help, be as specific as you can be so that there is no room for misinterpretation or misunderstanding.

- Apologizing while asking for help creates a feeling that you and the other person aren't on the same team, so try to avoid doing so excessively.

- Don't use disclaimers, either. When you are trying too hard to prove you are not greedy or weak, it adds a negative dimension to the conversation.

- Portraying the help you need as something insignificant or small also diminishes the effort that the other person would put in to meet your request. This prevents any warmth from developing as a result of one person's generosity and the other person's gracious acceptance of it.

- Even if you have actually done the person a favor in the past, don't mention it. Reminding them of it may make them feel obligated; thus, it won't be a genuine, heartfelt gesture on their part.

- Researchers have found that face-to-face requests are a lot likelier to receive a favorable response than requests made over text or email.

- Don't make your request transactional by mentioning how you'll return the favor.

- People love hearing good things about themselves. Just make sure that you are genuine with your words.

- You don't need to make someone indebted in order to increase your chances of receiving a favor from them. In fact, your chances of receiving a favor are much higher if you have already graciously received a favor from another person.

- Working on graciously receiving compliments is the first step toward opening your heart to receiving kindness from others. Next time someone pays you a compliment, reply with a heartfelt thank you.

- Let others share your load and make things a bit lighter for you. Again, all you need to do in return is to offer genuine praise and appreciation. Receive graciously—but always with gratitude and appreciation.

- Instead of trying to pay back for a gift, try paying forward. Bless someone else with your generosity and kindness.

Chapter 6
Sorting Through the Deceased Person's Belongings and Handling Awkward Comments

> When times are good, be grateful, and when times are tough, be graceful.
>
> —Dustin Poirier

The death of a loved one changes our lives and worlds forever. We find ourselves facing challenges that we couldn't have imagined encountering. There are so many things to take care of and so many responsibilities to attend after the death of someone significant in our lives. Unfortunately, none of us are handed a manual to understand how to respond to these challenging circumstances. In this chapter, I have done my best to provide you with answers to some of the most pressing questions and situations you may encounter.

What to Do with the Belongings of a Deceased Loved One

I think this is the hardest thing that we all have to deal with after the death of a loved one—the very real conundrum of what to do with their belongings. Going through their possessions can be a gut-wrenching experience that might bring up both good and bad memories. Having to make key decisions about what to do with those belongings can also serve as a final blow, reminding us that someone we loved dearly is no longer with us. I would strongly recommend that you seek the support of other family members or good friends while going through belongings, if possible.

Start When You're Ready

I know that this advice won't apply to everyone, as not every person will have the luxury of time to postpone sorting out the belongings of their deceased loved one. Maybe you are compelled to sell the house, or the rest of the family wants to or needs to get the task completed sooner rather than later. There can be a lot of reasons why you might have to do the sorting immediately after the death, but if you have the luxury of time, take advantage of it.

You may also feel more ready to sort through some things while keeping others for another time. After all, there may be things that require urgent attention and others that can wait. If you aren't feeling ready to sort the urgent things out, then ask for someone else to do it for you (if you are comfortable with that). In case you don't have that option available, or you just can't accept the idea of someone else doing it, then you can ask a loved one to be by your side for emotional support as you complete the task.

Asking Yourself Important Questions

Once you start sorting through your deceased loved one's belongings, figuring out what to do with them can feel very confusing and frustrating.

How Much Storage Space Do You Have?

The most important question you need to ask yourself is how much storage space you have. If you live in a small apartment and the deceased person had a large house where they lived by themselves, you may not have the space that's required to retain most of their belongings.

If that person was living with you and you plan to continue living in the same house, then you may not have to scale down their belongings right away or at all. However, it would be a good idea to donate or discard items that bring up negative or painful emotions. You can also bless someone else's life by donating belongings. But you don't have to do it if that's not what feels right in your heart. Listen to your heart and do what feels right to you. You don't have to do what others tell you or what's written in this book if your heart doesn't agree with it.

When tackling an intimate item like clothing, you can ask yourself questions like: Can I wear this? Will I actually wear it? Is there someone else in the family who would enjoy wearing it? Be honest with your answers, I know it's not easy. I kept a lot of my sister's cardigans thinking that I would wear them in the winter, but that never ended up happening. The truth was my sister had a very different sense of personal style than me. Even though I wanted to feel her presence by keeping her things around, they didn't have any practical purpose for me. Eventually, I ended up donating those cardigans. At the same time, I got a lot of use out of her cashmere scarves and I can never imagine giving them to someone else. Those scarves keep me warm in the winter—it is like having her symbolically next to me throughout the cold winter months. The memory of her unconditional love warms my heart while her scarves keep my body warm.

Also, it can be very confusing to figure out the correct answer right away. There is no hurry. If you are confused, keep the item with you. You can decide at a later date what you would like to do with them. But if you give everything away, there is no possibility of getting a chance to reconsider your decision. Besides, usually there are items that people like to keep with them just because it serves as a strong reminder of the deceased person and the beautiful relationship they had with them.

When working through other items like books, trinkets, memorabilia, furniture, photographs, jewelry, antiques, bathroom items, kitchen supplies, and so on, ask yourself if these items serve any functional and aesthetic value to you. As Marie Kondo would say, "Do they spark joy in your heart?"

If you start feeling guilty about letting something go, just remember your loved one would always want you to be happy. I'm sure they wouldn't want you to feel burdened by holding on to the things that don't bring a smile to your face or add value to your life in some way.

Important Items that You Should Keep

There are certain items that you should definitely keep for practical reasons.

Password Logs

If your loved one has a diary where they have listed all their passwords, or they were using a password manager that you are able to access, you need to hold on to it. These passwords will help you access their important documents that may be needed for a number of reasons.

Business-Related Documents

If your loved one owned a business or was involved in a business, you should preserve all their important business-related documents. This can include income/expense statements, payroll records, and the like. It would be a good idea to consult a business attorney for this, as there may be things that need to be done to either wrap up the business or transfer the deceased person's responsibilities to someone else.

Bank Accounts/Utility Bills/Home and Other Assets Ownership/Mortgage Documents

I know how intimidating it can be to go through these. In the aftermath of a death, there will be a lot of paperwork that needs to be dealt with. Make sure that all the accounts that won't be used anymore get closed, and you want to keep the proof of the closure with you. Some of the assets will be changing hands and there will be money that needs to be withdrawn. If you find all this overwhelming, ask for help from someone who is knowledgeable in these matters. Try to save all the paperwork, as you never know when they might be needed again in the future.

Passport and Other Identity-Related Documents

All identity-related documents should be preserved. Store them at the same place where you are keeping their death certificate. You may have to find these documents at some point to prove the deceased person's identity and your relationship to them for a number of reasons.

Tax Documents

You will want to hold on to these for at least three years. It is unlikely, but there might be a rare situation where you will need them. In my opinion, it is always better to be safe than sorry.

Retirement-Related Paperwork

If your loved one has retired, then it's a good idea to hold on to all their retirement paperwork. This can include pension slips, annuity contracts, and other such documents.

In general, my suggestion is that you try to preserve as much paperwork as you can. You never know what you'll end up needing. I know it can feel like a burden to save it all, especially because dealing with them often feels intimidating. I have one hack that I can share with you: I store all the things that I have to keep but don't bring joy to my heart in beautiful gift boxes. You can easily pick these boxes up online or at a local gift shop. This way, every time I look at the box, I feel joy and all the paperwork is safely stored inside without being in my face all the time.

Don't Feel Guilty about Getting Rid of Things

There's always some serious purging that needs to happen after the death of a loved one. Don't feel guilty about getting rid of items that don't bring you joy or that won't serve a utilitarian purpose for you. It is okay to not want to keep these things. I like to take a picture of each item before donating or selling, this way I will still have the memory with me forever. And that item won't be taking up any real estate in my home.

You can also consider making alternative uses out of items that you just can't get rid of. For instance, that special coffee mug which reminds you of your beloved can sit on your table as a penholder. Think creatively if you can figure out a way to use items in a new way that you'll enjoy.

Handling Awkward Comments from Others

Engaging in conversation with others after the death of a loved one can feel like walking through a minefield. You feel so raw and vulnerable; you are afraid of hearing certain things. And then the inevitable happens—someone says something that rubs you the wrong way.

It is important to understand that different people respond differently to death, loss, and grief. Just because the other person has said something you didn't like doesn't mean they wanted to hurt you.

I'm all for giving the benefit of the doubt to people. It is possible that the person wanted to comfort you and in their desire to do so, they couldn't figure out anything else to say. There's also the possibility that they are saying to you what they would themselves expect to hear from someone in your circumstances.

Since our needs can differ significantly from person to person, what works for someone else may not work for us, and vice versa. It is always best to focus on the intentions of the person than on their words and actions. Sometimes people say and do things we don't like with the best of intentions. Give them credit for their good intentions. As for their words and actions, here are some ideas on how to deal with them:

Be direct and upfront: If you didn't like what they said or did, tell them about it. Most of the time, people don't realize how their words or actions hurt us. Be honest about how you are feeling without finger-pointing or blaming them. For instance, don't say, "How could you say that to me?" Instead, you can say, "I feel very hurt when I hear words like that." Keep the focus on yourself and how you are feeling. When we blame someone or try to hold them responsible for how we are feeling, they are more likely to get defensive. People listen more intently and empathetically when we are sharing how we are feeling without making them responsible for it.

Change the subject: There may be certain situations where being upfront may not be the best strategy. So under those circumstances, you can simply change the subject. Try to subtly redirect the conversation to something more pleasant. I would suggest picking a subject of mutual interest so that the conversation can be engaging.

Discuss it later: If someone's comments leave you feeling unhinged and angry, it may be best to wait awhile before saying anything to them. In the heat of anger and emotional upheaval, we are likely to say things we'll regret later. When you are ready, tell the other person how you felt about their comments or actions. Again, focus on *I*-centric language. I know this can be really hard to do when we are convinced that the other person is the cause of our misery. But no one can make you miserable without your permission. Don't give your power away by thinking that anyone else in this world has that kind of power over you. Try to discuss with the other person what you didn't like, but don't count on them to change immediately, or at all. Either way, communicating your feelings about the matter will help you feel lighter. You'll also have the conviction that you tried your best to salvage your relationship with that person. There's also a fair chance that they may understand their mistake and apologize for it. I personally really believe in giving people second chances, especially if I know that their comments and actions were misguided attempts at being loving or they stemmed from plain ignorance. You'll be surprised how most of the time people have no idea how their words and actions are affecting us. When they realize their mistakes, most people genuinely make an effort to change.

Again, be kind and give others the benefit of the doubt. In most cases, people say the wrong things because they don't know any better and not because they intentionally want to hurt you.

Chapter Summary

- When going through the belongings of a deceased loved one, don't take home anything that you don't absolutely love. However, there may be things that remind you of good times shared with the deceased person. It is perfectly okay to hold on to them if you think you can give them an appropriate home at your place or safely store them.

- You need to hold on to password logs, business-related documents, account- and asset-related documents, identity-related documents, and retirement paperwork. Also, keep your loved one's tax-related documents for at least three years.

- Don't feel guilty about getting rid of items that don't bring you joy or that won't serve a utilitarian purpose. It is okay to not want to keep these things.

- When dealing with insensitive comments from others, it is best to focus on the intentions of the person instead of their words or actions. Sometimes people say and do things we don't like with the best of intentions.

- Very often people don't realize how their words or actions hurt us. Be honest about how you feel without finger-pointing or blaming them.

- There may be certain situations where being upfront may not be the best strategy. In those cases, simply change the subject. Try to subtly redirect the conversation to something more pleasant.

- If someone's comments leave you feeling unhinged and angry, it may be best to wait awhile before saying anything to them.

- When you don't feel comfortable telling the other person how you feel about their behavior, it would be a good idea to ask someone else to intervene on your behalf.

Chapter 7
Dealing With Grief Attacks and Keeping the Departed Soul Alive in Your Heart

> **Don't cry because it's over. Smile because it happened.**
>
> —Dr. Seuss

Grief is a complicated process. We don't experience it in a linear fashion. You may have arrived at an after-grief stage where your loss isn't the first thought on your mind when you wake up in the morning, or you aren't always feeling so raw that any mention of your departed loved one will cause you to break down in tears. Yet on your way home, you might turn the radio on in the car and there it is—the favorite song of your loved one playing. You experience an avalanche of emotions that suddenly makes you feel like you are back at square one.

You may wonder if you have grieved properly, or if your grieving is incomplete in some way. There is nothing wrong with the way you had grieved. Grief attacks are a normal phenomenon and they can happen even years after the death of a loved one.

You can't predict when, where, or if you'll suffer from them. But if it does happen to you, just remember it is a normal reaction to the death of someone who was close to you.

Days that Are Extra Hard

There are certain days when we can expect to feel swarmed by the memories of the deceased. This could be birthdays, anniversaries, or other special occasions that you used to share with them. When you know in advance that you will be missing your loved one, you can prepare for these occasions better.

Plan for It

Make a plan for how you'll be spending the day. On the first birthday of my sister after her death, I didn't make a plan. Every year we used to get together for a lunch that would turn into an evening soiree with friends and family. That year I was alone. I had not expected it to be as excruciatingly painful as it turned out to be. I had to take leave from work as I had started getting a sick feeling in my stomach. Once I got home, I just stayed in bed and cried all day and all night.

I would strongly suggest that you make a plan for these special occasions. Surround yourself with friends and family who truly care about you. Yes, one person you loved immensely is gone, but there are still quite a few other people who love you deeply and who mean a lot to you. Instead of seeing these occasions as days of mourning, start recognizing them as reasons to celebrate. Celebrate these days because your departed loved one's life and presence in this world are things worth celebrating. Even though they are gone, their life and memory lives on. You must celebrate and honor the life they had.

Come Up with Creative Ideas for Celebrating the Life of Your Departed Loved One

On the death anniversary of your loved one, think of creative ways in which you can celebrate them. Maybe you can host a dinner or lunch where everyone shares their best memories with the departed soul. Perhaps you can organize a picnic near the lake where their ashes were sprinkled.

You can also celebrate their death anniversary on your own, but I feel it's always a better idea to involve friends and family on such an occasion. You don't know what kind of thoughts and emotions might come up. Having other people around you will provide you with support you may need. Also, you'll enjoy listening to the stories others have to share about that person who is no longer with you.

Indulge in Self-Care

When tragedy hits us, our daily routines and schedules go for a toss. It becomes hard to remain committed to fitness and other self-care activities. I am very sure that your loved one wouldn't want you to be suffering, even if they are no longer in this world to tell you.

In their honor, do something that makes you feel good. Perhaps you can book yourself a day at the spa or attend a workshop that you long wanted to attend. Give yourself something that is truly special to you and will help you feel great—think of it as a gift from your loved one. I am sure they would do anything to put a smile on your face. So you must make yourself happy to honor their soul.

Start a Tradition

Traditions have a very important place in the human experience. They give us a sense of rootedness and provide a certain element of predictability to an otherwise chaotic experience of life. You can start a new tradition that will ensure that your loved one continues to live through it for a long time.

For instance, if everyone was accustomed to going over to Grandma's place for Thanksgiving, that tradition may get disrupted after her passing. But this can be replaced with a new tradition. Perhaps you can go and distribute some good food at the local hospice where she spent her last days and some of her friends may still be around. Just check in advance if the hospice is okay with accepting such help or you can think of some other way in which you can bring a smile to other people's face.

My sister used to love peonies. Every autumn, I add a new peony plant to my garden. Every time I see those beautiful flowers blooming in my garden, I get reminded of the ever-smiling and cheerful face of my sister.

Think of something that is meaningful and special to you, then add it to your own personal tradition or turn it into a family tradition (if everyone is onboard with it).

Support Groups

Joining a support group that has other members dealing with similar challenges can be very helpful. These days, you can easily find such groups with an online search. If that's not an option, then you can check with your local hospice or funeral home. Joining a support group can be a profoundly healing experience. You are likely to find someone who understands you since there are so many people grieving the loss of a loved one—at least one person will have a grieving style similar to yours.

Keeping the Departed Soul Alive in Your Heart

Death may mark the end of a relationship but it doesn't have to imply an end to love. You can keep the departed soul alive in your heart for the rest of your life. Letting go doesn't mean letting go of love. Moving on is a process of overcoming all the negative emotions and pain associated with the demise of your loved one. This doesn't mean you have to erase them from your memory. It is impossible to forget someone who held a special place in our heart.

Here are some ideas for how you can keep your loved one alive in your heart forever:

Keep Meaningful Items with You

Keep meaningful items with you to remind you of the good times you had with your loved one, or to simply remind you of their presence. It can be anything—from a special key chain they bought on a trip to Paris, to a jumper they loved wearing through the winter season. It can even be something much bigger, like their favorite study table. In the midst of grief, it can be quite tempting to get rid of all the belongings of the departed soul, especially when the pain of missing them becomes unbearable. Don't do it—wait for a while and there will likely be some items that you'll want to keep for yourself.

Think About the Advice They Would Give You if They Were Around

Before taking any big decisions, think of the advice or opinion that your loved one would give you. Even though they are not physically around anymore, they are still very much alive in your heart. Trust me, once you have formed a bond with someone, a part of them will always live in you. So whenever you ask your heart for guidance about what your loved one would say to you in that moment, you are always going to receive an answer. You just have to listen keenly and attentively—the voice of the heart is often subtle but clear.

Share their Stories with Others

Talk about your loved one to people who knew them, as well as those who may not have met them but might have appreciated knowing them. Make sure that their legacy continues by sharing the stories and results of their good deeds with as many people as possible.

Live Your Life in a Manner that Would Make Them Proud

There is no greater act of love than honoring your departed loved one and living in a way that would make them proud. Before taking any important step, ask yourself if what you are about to do would make your loved one proud or not. Try to do more of those things that would definitely make them proud.

Finish Their Incomplete Projects

Was there something that your loved one was working on prior to their death? Maybe it was a kitchen renovation, a charity event they wanted to organize, or perhaps even a fun craft project. This is your chance to complete their incomplete tasks. You'll find a very interesting and strange sense of peace by doing this. After my sister died, I realized that she had all these Christmas cards on her study table that she was planning to send to all her friends and family. I decided to send them on her behalf. While it may seem a little strange to receive Christmas wishes on behalf of someone who is no longer in this world, it was deeply comforting to everyone who received a card. They got beautiful memorabilia to cherish for the rest of their lives, and they also got to know that my sister had them on her mind even when she was going through her personal struggles.

Do Something from Their Bucket List

If there was something that your loved one was really keen on doing, then perhaps you should do it now. It could be that trip to Alaska they always wanted to take to watch the Northern Lights, or maybe jumping off a plane to skydive. Pick something that you yourself would like to experience. You may end up missing them sorely, but you'll also find comfort in knowing that you got to live and experience something on their behalf. You'll find peace in knowing that through you, your loved one was able to live and experience something that really mattered to them.

Chapter Summary

- Grief attacks are a normal phenomenon and they can happen even years after the death of a loved one. You can't predict them. But if it does happen to you, just remember it is a normal reaction to the death of someone who was close to you.

- Make a plan for how you'll spend special occasions. Celebrate these days because your departed loved one's life and presence in this world is something worth celebrating. Even though they are gone, their life and memory lives on.

- On the death anniversary of your loved one, think of creative ways in which you can celebrate them, give yourself something that is truly special to you, or work with family to create a new tradition.

- Before taking any big decision, think of the advice or opinion that your loved one will give you. Try to live in a way that would make them proud.

- Talk about your loved one to people who knew them and to those who may not have met them, but would have appreciated knowing them.

- If there was a project that your loved one was working on before their death, consider completing it on their behalf.

- If there was something that your loved one was really keen on doing (like a bucket list item), then try doing it for them now.

Vanessa's Story
An Inspiring Account of Hope and Healing

I met Vanessa while volunteering at the local hospital. We were both working with terminally ill patients—doing our best to give comfort, solace, and some joy to those who were fighting for their survival every day of their lives. It wasn't easy by any means; we struggled to smile while facing death every moment of the day. The most difficult aspect of this job was when, on some mornings, we walked in and learned that a patient with whom we had developed a special bond had passed away at night or early in the morning. It was gut-wrenching, being so painfully aware how fragile the thread of life really is.

There was no time to take anything for granted. We were always conscious of the fact that the person we were sharing a smile with may not be around when we walked into the hospital the next day. This experience did make me extremely grateful for all that I had, and most of all for the love that I had been blessed with in my life.

But truth be told, even though I was volunteering at a hospital for terminally ill patients, I was struggling with my own demons every single day. Losing my sister had left me with a void that nothing in the world could fill. She was my best friend, my soulmate—the one person in the world with whom I could share anything and everything.

Even though I was living a truly blessed life in so many ways, it was becoming increasingly hard for me to look at the glass half full. Most of the time I was lost in memories of the past and I thought of the future with dread. I felt so broken that I did not know how I could go on for another year. The future looked like a black blob of nothingness that evoked a deep sense of fear and dread. While on the surface it looked like I was doing something good by helping out the terminally ill patients in whatever way I could, the truth was I needed them more than they needed me. By helping them, I was helping myself. When I was able to bring a smile to their faces, I found myself smiling. Also, most importantly, I felt that by helping them I was doing something for my sister who had died of cancer a few years ago.

Vanessa was different. When you looked at her it seemed like she didn't have a care in the world. She was deeply compassionate and tender toward all the patients and always cheerful. She had a smile that could light up a room, literally and figuratively. It really was as bright and radiant as the sun shining on a beautiful spring afternoon.

To be honest, I felt a slight sense of envy. What was her secret? How did she manage to be so happy all the time? How could she be so compassionate and yet so detached at the same time? These were only some of the questions that would baffle me every day. To make myself feel better, I had concluded that perhaps she'd had a privileged life. Or maybe she hadn't known any real hardships of her own, considering that she was only thirty and it seemed everything was going well for her in life.

I really wanted to find out what Vanessa's secret was. I genuinely wanted to have her sense of positivity and cheerfulness, but didn't know how. When I couldn't contain my curiosity anymore, I decided to just ask her: "Vanessa, how do you manage to stay so cheerful all the time? You are so compassionate and caring, I see tears in your eyes when a patient passes on. But after a while you always get back to your cheerful self. What is your secret?"

Vanessa looked at me with warmth and love in her eyes. "I take life as it comes. No matter what is happening in the world around us, there is always something to be grateful for. I see the blessing in every situation no matter what. I love deeply but without attachments. Most people think that love and attachment are the same, but they are not. Attachment is born out of our selfish desires; true love is completely unconditional. I choose to love unconditionally and I trust the process of life—the ebb and flow, the highs and lows—that's why I am always at peace."

I was really intrigued by Vanessa's answer but I can't say I fully understood what she was saying. Indeed, I understood the words but I wasn't able to comprehend the depth and wisdom contained in them because I was personally not at a place where I could claim to have found that kind of peace and happiness. Perhaps even my experience of unconditional love wasn't complete. I had so much attachment to my sister. I wasn't willing to let go of it, because letting go felt as if I was going to stop loving her.

I mulled over Vanessa's words and looked intently at her. There was something really remarkable and extraordinary about that young woman. She was so gentle, yet she seemed so strong. She was busy helping out a seventy-year-old patient who had been fighting stage four cancer for the last several months. He was very weak and looked painfully skeletal. Vanessa had this ability to make him smile even in the midst of the health catastrophe he was facing. She would playfully tease him and sometimes even scold him as if he were a little boy and she was his mother. He loved being babied by her and those were the times when I would see this radiant smile beaming on his face. There was something so innocent and beautiful about that smile on his weak face. The only other time I had seen him smile like that was when his four-year-old granddaughter would come visit.

Vanessa was highly intuitive. She could sense from the look on my face that I was intrigued and wanted to know more. She turned and said to me, "We can talk over coffee sometime if you want."

I said, "I would love that. I am free tomorrow afternoon at three if that works for you?"

She said, "Yes, that works for me. Let's meet at three at Joe's Coffeehouse."

The next day, I showed up fifteen minutes early to Joe's Coffeehouse. To my surprise, Vanessa was already there. She said, "I know you're always early. I feel we have a lot to talk about so I'm here."

I smiled at her and said, "Indeed, I really need some wisdom from you. How do you stay so positive all the time?"

Vanessa replied, "Sheila, I know you have been through a lot. It's not easy seeing the glass half full when you have lost someone who was dear to your heart. Trust me, I wasn't always like this. I have had to choose to be the person that I am."

And then she went on to tell me her story, which I am going to share with you here. I hope it inspires you just as much as it inspired me then, and continues to inspire me now.

Vanessa Hodges was born in a small town in Texas called Marfa. Her mother had several affairs and she had a serious drinking problem. Her father was a hardworking man who struggled to make ends meet, and with just as much of a drinking problem as Vanessa's mother. Vanessa's earliest memories were of violent fights between her mother and father. Sometimes those fights happened while they were sober, but most of the time they happened in the aftermath of being drunk like a fish. Her father often accused Vanessa's mother of being a harlot. It seemed like the fights would get worse whenever one of his coworkers—especially Mr. Sanchez—would pay a visit to Vanessa's home when her father wasn't around. At the time, Vanessa didn't know what *harlot* meant or why her parents were always at each other's throats.

Vanessa was usually terrified of the environment at home. She dreaded returning from school, as she couldn't predict what she was going to find at her place. Most of the time, she would hide in the attic trying to mentally escape to a better place where everyone was happy and at peace. Unfortunately, peace and happiness eluded Vanessa to such an extent that she started wondering if she had been cursed.

While her parents fought night after night, Vanessa had her own secrets to hide and demons to fight. When her mother would be busy around the house or she wasn't around, Mr. Sanchez would find Vanessa hiding in the attic. The first time he touched her she tried to run. She could see something in his eyes that felt scary—he had these reddish eyes that would ogle at her as if he was a monster hunting his prey. And then the molestation began.

Vanessa was obviously too young to understand what was going on, but she knew that something didn't feel right. One day she decided to tell her mother about it. "Mom, I don't like Mr. Sanchez."

Her mother replied with a taunt, "Why?"

Vanessa replied, "The other day he touched me. I didn't like it."

What happened next wasn't something Vanessa had expected. Vanessa's mother planted a tight slap on her cheek. It was such a hard blow that Vanessa fell down to her side. Her mother said, "Don't lie to me ever again. I don't understand how you make up such nonsense, you disgusting little vermin! Don't you dare utter such nonsense in front of your father!"

Vanessa was utterly shocked. She felt lonely and despondent. Her own mother didn't believe her words. She wouldn't dare tell her father about it. It seemed like he already hated it whenever he found out that Mr. Sanchez had come over to their house behind his back. She wasn't sure how bad the situation at home would get if she shared her story with him. Besides, she wasn't sure if he would even believe her.

Vanessa fell into an intense depression. She was regularly bullied at school, as some of the kids caught word of her mother's affairs. Vanessa was constantly called names and teased about it. She felt terribly lonely and often wondered what the point of living was when life was so tormentous and painful everywhere she turned. Once she became a teenager, Vanessa found solace in reading romance novels. She fantasized that there was a man who would love her and understand her. She'd finally get her happily after—the peaceful family life she had always dreamt of.

When she was around sixteen years old, she met Liam. He was a handsome man of twenty who used to work at the local hardware shop, where they met. Liam and Vanessa instantly started liking each other. Vanessa had gone to the store to buy some supplies for her dad. The moment Vanessa saw Liam, she started feeling that her dream of a handsome prince swaying her off her feet and taking all her problems away could come true.

Eventually, Liam asked her out and their whirlwind romance began. By the time she was eighteen, Vanessa had married Liam, whom she believed was her knight in shining armor. However, it only took a few months of being married to realize that her life was falling short of being a fairy tale.

After the marriage, Liam turned into a completely different man than the one she had dated. The old Liam was caring and kind. The new Liam bossed her around and hardly ever cared about what she liked or disliked. A year into the marriage, she realized that Liam was cheating on her.

Despite being cheated on, Vanessa thought that maybe her love could redeem the relationship. She thought she was loving him unconditionally by letting him do as he pleased and not uttering a word of protest, no matter how unfairly he treated her. Liam's behavior continued to get more and more monstrous, while Vanessa's tolerance toward the abuse grew in proportion. One day, Liam told her, "I'm done Vanessa. I can't do this anymore. I'm in love with Mia."

Vanessa begged him to not leave her. She even pleaded with him to stay with her—he could have a relationship with Mia on the side and she would still love him. As pathetic as that sounds, Vanessa was ready to do anything to save the one relationship where she had found some semblance of love. However, Liam left her crying on the kitchen floor. He walked out of the door with two suitcases and never came back.

Vanessa eventually sold the house and moved to another city. She didn't have a child and she wanted to start fresh. She started working two jobs while studying at the local community college. Even though

Vanessa was heartbroken, she still hoped to find true love—that one man who could redeem her from her past.

Vanessa met several men over the years and the same story played out every time. Finally, she met a man named Roger. He treated her with love, respect, and care. Within a few months of dating, the two got married and for the first time in her life, Vanessa felt truly happy. She had a lot of fear and insecurity because of her troubled past, but Roger supported her in every way he could.

Unfortunately, their blissful marriage didn't last long. One October evening, Vanessa received a phone call that left her devastated. Roger had died in a car accident. The one man who had given her what she had been craving her entire life was now gone. She felt that with him, all her dreams and hopes had died.

Vanessa couldn't eat for days. She just stayed in bed and cried all day and night. As the months went by, Vanessa felt increasingly depressed and suicidal. She really felt that she couldn't go on another day. Her doctor agreed to prescribe her some sleeping pills so that she could get some rest. Vanessa craved to feel at peace, or maybe even to just feel nothing for once.

Thanks to the long-term effects of those sleeping pills, her brain began to become increasingly dull. She lacked alertness and sharpness of mind while performing even simple everyday tasks.

One day, Vanessa felt she'd had enough. She thought the one man who had loved her was no longer in this world. What was the point of going on? She felt she belonged with him and not on this earthly plane where no one had ever really loved her except Roger.

On a whim, Vanessa took her car keys and started driving. She wasn't sure where she was going but as soon as she got on an empty road, she hit the gas pedal hard. It was raining heavily and she wasn't able to see anything on the road. In the moment, she felt as if time had stopped—all thoughts started disappearing and she was simply present in a vacuum of time and space. The next thing she saw was a flash of her entire life before her eyes. She realized there was so much still left in this world for her to experience. She didn't want to die, because she truly wanted to experience it all. It's just that she was in so much pain that she felt death could be the only thing that brought her some relief. But what she truly wanted was a better life—one filled with love and laughter.

After that, Vanessa remembered nothing. When she woke up, she was in the hospital. She had severely injured her legs in the accident. The doctors weren't sure if Vanessa would be able to walk again. Something interesting happened at that moment. All the pain and suffering faded in comparison to the gut-wrenching agony that came with realizing she would no longer be able to walk or use her body in the same way again. She begged God, or whatever higher power there was, to give her legs back—she would live every day with gratitude; she would value all her blessings.

Vanessa also realized that she truly wanted to live. Indeed, she had loved Roger deeply, but perhaps he was meant to have a set amount of time in her life. She was still so young—Vanessa craved having a family with a man who would love her and cherish her for the rest of her life. But more than anything, she craved to have her body back. At that point Vanessa resolved to work hard to change her life completely. Dying wasn't an option anymore. She had to live, and if she must live then she'd better make the best out of it.

Through sheer resolve and hard work, Vanessa regained the use of her legs. Even the doctors were surprised by what she had managed to accomplish—it was a medical miracle.

This experience made Vanessa deeply grateful for all the blessings she had in her life—most of all, the blessing of a beautiful and wonderful body that helped her traverse the landscape of life. We take our bodies for granted, never pausing to thank them, but we are quick to complain when they have aches and pains due to our negligent and—a lot of the time, even abusive—attitudes toward our bodies.

Vanessa gave up sleeping pills and everything else that was destructive to her health and well-being. She resolved to be happy and worked hard for it. She devoured self-help books and attended innumerable seminars.

In the process of overcoming the extreme challenges she had faced, Vanessa blossomed into the finest version of herself. Even at a young age, she was wise beyond her years. She loved deeply, but understood that you could never make someone else the source of your happiness. She trusted that only God, or the universe, was her source of happiness. Vanessa had also made peace with the process of life. Life and death were two sides of the same coin. The beauty of life lies in its temporal nature. Indeed, all relationships are transitory as well. Why not love others as best as we can while they are here? When they are gone, we can find peace in knowing we did all we could to give them everything we could offer.

Vanessa also mentioned that she had come to realize that it is God, or the universe, that loves us through all the people we hold dear to our hearts. Our loved ones are like droplets in the infinite ocean of God's love. Even when the droplets merge back into the ocean, God's love never ceases to exist. This is why, as we move forward in life, we always end up meeting new people who love us and care for us. There is never any shortage of love—we just have to continue believing in it. Not the type of love that seeks to make someone else its source, but the type that sets the other person completely free.

I listened to Vanessa's story in awe. I had tears in my eyes as I thought about all the extremes that such a beautiful young woman had gone through. If she could face so much and come out being a kinder, wiser, and more loving person, then so could I. I also realized that I did love life—I'd thought I couldn't go on, but that wasn't the same as saying I did not want to live. I just wanted to live a happy life filled with love and laughter. And then this thought came to me: I was sure my sister wanted the same for me!

Conclusion

I really hope that this book has provided you with the solace and guidance you have been seeking. Grief is often such a lonely experience—we end up feeling like nobody understands us or that we are completely alone in our suffering. I hope by now you are able to truly understand the individual differences that cause people, even those in the same family, to grieve completely differently.

Don't treat this book as a one-time read that sits on a dusty shelf. Treat it more like a friend you keep coming back to for advice. In those times, when you are feeling overwhelmed by the pain and suffering that has come upon you due to this irreparable loss, I am sure that turning to this book will help you discover the answers that you seek. This is the book that I needed for myself when I was grieving the death of my sister. I couldn't find the answers that I needed anywhere. That's why I want to give you what I once desperately needed for myself, so that you don't have to face the same confusion or lack of guidance that I did.

I also want to urge you to be gentle and kind to yourself. It takes time to heal from emotional pain. Don't be too hard on yourself by always wondering when you'll be able to get back to normal again. Every person is different. There is really no tangible answer I can give you. As long as you are doing the work, you are improving—that's what really matters.

Also, the end of your earthly relationship with your departed loved one doesn't indicate the end of love itself. The love that you experienced with them will live in your heart forever. Both the love you gave and the love you received is yours to hold on to for eternity. They may not be physically around anymore, but their essence is going to live in you forever.

Let the departure of your dear one be a reminder to live every day with gratitude. Never take anything or anyone for granted. Our lives are so profoundly blessed—we always have so much to be thankful for, even on those days when we think nothing is going right. I am sure that you took your loved one for granted a lot of times when they were around. We all do it.

I know how deep your pain is, but I also want to remind you that there are other people in your life right now who you love and who love you deeply. Don't forget to cherish them. Talk to them about your heart's truest desires—share your thoughts and feelings. In the grand scheme of things, all relationships are just a brief temporal experience, but the impression they leave on our consciousness lasts an eternity.

The departed soul is no longer with you, but a part of their soul has merged with you forever. From now on, whenever you find yourself thinking about them, bring a smile to your face and think about all the ways in which they enriched your life. Celebrate them and their life in whatever way you can. They were here for a purpose and a reason. Now that they are gone, their legacy must live forever!

I Need Your Help . . .

I want to thank you for putting your trust in me. I hope this book has helped you in healing from grief. I know it's not easy. But with time and effort, all wounds heal. Your loved one is always going to remain in your heart and soul. It's the pain of separation and the disappointment of having to carry on without them that must be relinquished.

This is the book that I wish I had when I was coping with the loss of my sister. But then, the pain of not knowing what I should do to heal from the loss and suffering that had besieged me from all sides is what eventually led me to creating this book. It is my dream and my vision to help millions of people across the globe who are dealing with grief. If you know someone who would benefit from this book, then please share it with them.

Also, I would like to ask you for a small favour. If you have found this book helpful, then please leave a review on Amazon. It would help other readers understand what they can expect from reading this book.

For any questions or feedback please feel free contacting me at: sheila@publish-master.com, I would love to hear from you!

http://publish-master.activehosted.com/f/1

Printed in Poland
by Amazon Fulfillment
Poland Sp. z o.o., Wrocław
09 January 2026

abd79e41-5a0e-40d6-91fa-3354bc929875R01